Mary Elizabeth Braddon

Sir Jasper's tenant

Mary Elizabeth Braddon

Sir Jasper's tenant

ISBN/EAN: 9783741197475

Manufactured in Europe, USA, Canada, Australia, Japa

Cover: Foto ©Andreas Hilbeck / pixelio.de

Manufactured and distributed by brebook publishing software (www.brebook.com)

Mary Elizabeth Braddon

Sir Jasper's tenant

SIR JASPER'S TENANT

BY THE AUTHOR OF

"LADY AUDLEY'S SECRET"

ETC. ETC. ETC.

IN THREE VOLUMES

VOL. II.

LONDON
JOHN MAXWELL AND COMPANY
122 FLEET STREET
M DCCC LXV

[All rights reserved]

CONTENTS OF VOL. II.

CHAP.		PAGE
I.	Dorothy's Engagement	1
II.	The Widow tears herself away	22
III.	Did he love her?	53
IV.	Miss Denison's Humiliation	75
V.	Farewell	101
VI.	The Story of a young Man's Folly	110
VII.	A Broken Life	138
VIII.	"And yet my Days go on, go on"	246
IX.	Twopenny-Postman	264

SIR JASPER'S TENANT

CHAPTER I.

DOROTHY'S ENGAGEMENT.

THE arbitrary baker who dealt out his customers' dinners like a pack of cards at a given hour, and thereby obliged Mr. Dobb to dine at one o'clock on a Sunday, exercised no influence upon that gentleman's domestic arrangements for the rest of the day; and on almost every Sunday evening throughout the year the brewer's clerk was wont to entertain his friends in a manner which was as economical as it was primitive. No troublesome preparations, to be achieved with wailing and gnashing of teeth by Mrs. Dobb, were involved in Henry Adolphus's "Sundays;"

no bewildering arithmetical calculation of spoons and forks, dessert-knives and carvers, finger-glasses and salt-cellars, had to be gone through by that lady. No occasional butler, proprietor of a neighbouring milk-walk, had to be consulted as to *his* engagements before the guests could be bidden. The "at home" of an early settler in the Australian bush could scarcely have been more unceremonious than Mr. Dobb's mode of entertaining his friends.

At an uncertain hour after the clearing away of the tea-things the clerk's little circle began to assemble. It was always the same circle, and it always gathered in the same manner; and what it did on one Sunday, it did on almost every Sunday through the year. As the winter dusk deepened into darkness, as the summer sunset darkened into dusk, Mr. Dobb's masculine acquaintance dropped in at Amanda Villas, and settled themselves for a pleasant evening. In the clerk's circle there was a good deal understood by the phrase "dropping in." It meant that costume was looser in its regulations than the

Duke de Bassano would quite approve of in the guests he invites to his imperial master's mansion. It meant that coloured waistcoats and flaming neckties were admissible; it meant unlimited indulgence from Mrs. Dobb in the matter of smoking. It even went so far as to mean the toleration of shirt-sleeves in very warm weather; and it meant a financial system with regard to refreshment and tobacco, which Mr. Dobb alluded to briefly as "Yorkshire," but which has been made familiar to us in that Scottish drinking-song called "Auld lang syne," wherein the noblest spirit of good-fellowship seems to be embodied in the rule that every man should pay his own score.

The refreshment which Mr. Dobb's visitors affected was half-and-half. When the four or five droppers-in who constituted the clerk's circle had assembled, the maid-of-all-work was despatched to the nearest tavern for a gallon of half-and-half, and to the nearest tobacconist's for a quarter of a pound of bird's-eye. Mr. Dobb, as a brewer's-clerk and a family-man, had a cask of XX from the brewery for his household consumption; but Mr. Dobb, in the character of Amphitryon, preferred the half-and-half procured for ready money from the tavern; for the "Yorkshire" system would have been clumsy in its application to beer supplied from the entertainer's private cellar, and might have entailed long credits and even bad debts. When the domestic returned from her mission, the can of half-and-half was placed in the centre of Mr. Dobb's round-table, and an array of blown-glass tumblers ranged at its base; the bird's-eye circulated amongst the guests in a jam-pot; and the evening's entertainment commenced. The evening's entertainment appeared to consist chiefly in the consumption of the beer and bird's-eye. Sometimes the maid-of-all-work was despatched for a second gallon; very frequently she had to fetch fresh supplies of tobacco; although every one of Mr. Dobb's visitors carried in his waistcoat-pocket a fragment of a black-looking compound, which he chopped or scraped solemnly at intervals to mingle with his bird's-eye, and which he called Cavendish. The capacity which Mr. Dobb and his friends displayed for the consumption of beer was something startling. They were not particularly thirsty; and the half-and-half, always growing gradually flatter as the evening waned, was by no means particularly nice; but the visitors imbibed glass after glass of the beverage with as solemn a relish as if the muddy-brown mixture in their tumblers had been the rarest vintage of the Rhine. With beer and tobacco Mr. Dobb's acquaintance seemed to find a perennial charm in his society. Without beer and tobacco they could not endure him for a moment: for it happened sometimes that the guests, unmindful of the hour, allowed the public-house to close before they had renewed their supplies; and lo, suddenly, when the genial spirit of good fellowship was at its brightest, the tin bottom of the can revealed itself glimmering through a swiftly-ebbing tide of half-and-half, and the revellers were fain to part sad and despondent. To have continued their conversation, to have sung another song or listened to another recitation, or to have lingered together in friendly intercourse for another half-hour *without* beer, would have been an impossibility; and the guests departed, determined to keep a sharper look-out upon the can and the hour next time. Sometimes when Mr. Dobb was in an expansive humour, he would ask his friends to partake of the cold baked meats remaining from his family-table, unlimited pickles of a very vinegary character, and a stale half-quartern; but this did not happen very often; for the boldest masculine spirit will quail before the settled blackness on a female visage, when Monday's dinner disappears before the ravages of unconscious Sunday visitors.

Little Dorothy Tursgood, spending a Sabbath holiday very often with her cousin Selina, had frequently enjoyed the privilege of joining in the Sunday-evening festivities. Country cousins are convenient people to know; and Selina Dobb found her civilities to Dorothy very advantageously requited by an occasional basket from the home-farm; and then Selina liked to hear all about Miss Marcia, and what she did, and what she wore, and what her bonnets cost; and what the parlour-dinners were like at the Abbey; and whether Sir Jasper was going to leave off living like a hermit; and so on. Dorothy was always welcome whenever her indulgent mistress was pleased to give her a Sunday's holiday; it being understood that she was to be seen safely back to the Abbey by the Dobbs, or fetched by her father, and that she was to return at a certain hour.

Until very lately Dorothy had been quite resigned to leaving the festive circle at rather an early period. The atmosphere created by so many clay pipes was rather trying, and Dorothy found very little amusement in the society of half-a-dozen solemn young men, or in the stereotyped witticisms of Henry Adolphus. But latterly Dorothy had found the tobacco-laden atmosphere of the crowded little parlour as delightful as the perfumed air of an earthly paradise. Latterly Dorothy had found even Mr. Dobb's jokes amusing: or she had at least found it amusing to listen to some one else, whose subdued accents were not heard by the general company during the laughter that followed the clerk's sallies. Of late Mr. Gervoise Catheron, the sub-lieutenant of marines, had been an occasional dropper-in at Amanda Villas: and by an odd coincidence his occasional droppings-in always happened to occur upon the evenings which Dorothy spent with her cousin. He came on those evenings because he knew that she was there. He watched her as she left the chapel, and found out all about it. He told her so; and he told her that he loved her very dearly, and that no other woman should be his wife. He was only waiting to turn himself round, he said, and to get out of this beastly corps, and get something to live upon, and then he would ask her to marry him immediately: and he did not care a—something very wicked, at which Dorothy gave a pretty little scream, and put her dumpling hands over his mouth—what his family or his friends might choose to say about any inequality of rank between the Catherons and the Tursgoods.

"What the deuce is the good of your old family, that they should make such a howling about it?" demanded Mr. Catheron peevishly. "Will your old family keep you? If it would,

I'd say something to it. Will your old family pay your debts? not a bit of it. I've heard my father say that in his time the King's Bench was peopled with old families; and the more certain it was that a man's ancestors came over with William the Conqueror, the more likely the man himself was to die in the Rules. Our family can trace itself back to the reign of Edward the Confessor; and a precious deal of good we get out of him, when we've bothered our brains to work ourselves back to him. If we could fasten the other end of our family on to a rich cotton-spinner or a wealthy iron-founder, we might get some recompense for our trouble; but if I wanted to do a little bit of stiff to-morrow, and Edward the Confessor could come out of his grave to put his name to it, his stupid old signature wouldn't be worth the paper it was written upon—even if he could write, which I haven't the faintest doubt he couldn't, since the other fellow, William the what's-his-name, never got beyond Bill Stokes his mark. So when I marry, Dorothy, I shall please myself, and Edward the Confessor may be—"

The dumpling hand went up to arrest the utterance of another wicked word, and then Dorothy trotted along beside her lover proud and happy. He acted as Mr. Dobb's proxy sometimes, and escorted her to the gates of Searsdale Park; for Selina had been taken into Dorothy's confidence, and knew that her cousin and the sub-lieutenant were engaged. She had even heard as much from the lips of that gentleman himself, who declared his intentions to be strictly honourable, but who begged that they might not be revealed to Mr. Dobb, who was a "talking fellow, and would be likely to go blabbing the business all over Castleford," Mr. Catheron said.

So Dorothy was engaged. The lieutenant's declaration had come very soon, and yet she did not think that it had come abruptly; for a new existence seemed to have dawned for her since the day when she had first seen him looking at her in the humble little chapel: and now when she tried to remember what her life had been like without him, she lost herself in the effort to recall that bygone time, until it seemed as if she could have had no existence at all before that never-to-be-forgotten day. All that had gone before was so dim and faded, that she could not seize the memory of a single hour out of all her life, until the bright moment in which her heart first fluttered with so sweet an emotion that she had never even tried to still its altered beating, or to coax it back to the old jog-trot pace.

And yet Mr. Catheron was as commonplace a lover as ever said commonplace things in a commonplace way. But then he was Dorothy's first lover, and he had all the benefit of that wondrous glamour which belongs to new emotions kindled in a fresh young heart. His compliments might be dull and hackneyed; but they were the first that had ever brought the warm blushes to Dorothy's cheeks. From him she heard for the first time that hazel eyes and rosy lips are agreeable objects, for the love of which Edward the Confessor himself might be cast to the winds. It was he who informed her that she had dimples, and that dimples were nice things to have. He might be commonplace; but then he did not present himself before Dorothy in his own person. It was not the dissolute, shiftless, penniless sub-lieutenant of marines whom the bailiff's daughter met in that smoky parlour: it was Love,—the ever young and ever beautiful; the radiant divinity, beneath whose influence Titania can see perfection in the ass's head of a village joiner; whose breath exhales from the lips of Pyramus whispering through the chink in the wall, and transforms the boy's most vulgar words into the murmurs of a demigod. It was the same divinity who visited Dido in the guise of Æneas, and shone upon Telemachus out of the bewildering eyes of Calypso. What matters the disguise in which the god chooses to veil his divinity? Change as he may, his power is still the same, and is still no part of the shape he bears; but his own, and his own only. Louis la Vallière may limp, but Love is not lame. The shrinking violet may be marked with the small-pox, but Eros is affected by no mortal malady. It is only when the Protean divinity changes his disguise, and skips into the earthly semblance of Athénée de Montespan, or frolics in the ribbon-bound locks of De Fontanges, that the king discovers how his poor penitent Louise was no such dazzling beauty; and then the celestial boy, half-imp, half-angel, enshrines himself in the portly figure of a comely middle-aged widow, and, tired of so many transformations, the divine spirit is content to hold his new shape, and prim De Maintenon's eyes shine on her benefactor with a flame that is as steady as it is feeble. Surely sometimes, when he groaned over his troubles in the agreeable society of his second wife, the mighty Bourbon's fancies must have wandered back to the old, old days when Cupid bore the shape of Mazarin's beautiful niece, and the alias of Love was Mancini.

Dorothy had met the god in a shabby uniform and doubtful varnished boots; but the aureole of his divinity encircles his head, let him appear under what shape he will. If any body had told the bailiff's daughter that the Apollo was better-looking than Gervoise Catheron, that De Lauzun was more elegant, or De Grammont better bred, or Dr. Samuel Johnson better informed, she would only have shrugged her pretty little shoulders in ineffable contempt for that person's bad taste. She was engaged; and to a gentleman. Her little head swam with the intoxication of this last idea. Yes; Edward the Confessor had more to do with it than Mr. Catheron was aware of. He was a gentleman, of an old family. Dorothy had heard enough of old families, and quarterings, and intermarriages, and pedigrees that could be traced back to the dark ages before the Conquest. She had heard all this sort of thing discussed gravely by Mrs. Browning, the housekeeper at the Abbey; and the foolish little heart swelled to bursting as she thought how delicious it would be to change the odious name of Tursgood—a name shared with cousins who were blacksmith's apprentices and with uncles who couldn't write—for the high-sounding appellation of Catheron.

That her lover was a poverty-stricken scamp, who borrowed half-sovereigns of Mr. Dobb, and had to be reminded of their loan before he returned them, was a fact that made no impression whatever upon Dorothy's mind. Charles Stuart hiding for hours at a stretch in the branches of an oak; or scudding across country disguised as an agricultural labourer; or crossing the Channel in Captain Tattersall's boat, could scarcely have been the most heroic object, looked upon by uninitiated eyes; but he was King Charles the Second of Great Britain and Ireland nevertheless, and the divinity which hedges even kings who are down in the world encircled him still. So Gervoise Catheron, borrowing half-sovereigns and wearing doubtful boots, was only a prince under a cloud, and bore the stamp of his Saxon descent inscribed in unmistakable characters upon his noble brow; at least so Dorothy thought; and Dorothy and his creditors were about the only people who did think of Gervoise Catheron. The lieutenant's physiognomy was rather of the Celtic than the Germanic type; and his dark eyes and hair indicated the introduction of southern blood in the line of his Saxon progenitors; but a complexion cannot be expected to last for the best part of a thousand years; and Dorothy concluded any little mental argument she held about her lover's personal appearance by declaring to herself that whatever Edward the Confessor might have been like, Gervoise Catheron was a great deal handsomer than any old Saxon monarch who ever lived upon this earth.

She would like to have told her generous mistress of her engagement; but the lieutenant forbade any such revelation.

"There's a person staying at the Abbey who knows me," Gervoise said; "and if it were to get to her ears, there'd be the deuce to pay; though why there should, or why I should consider *her* in the business when I never get any thing out of her, I don't know," concluded the lieutenant, who never was in one mind about the smallest thing for two minutes together, and whose conversation was positively bespattered with daresays and perhapses, and every phrase in the vocabulary indicative of indecision. "However, you'd better not tell her," concluded Mr. Catheron, "because, you see, you can do that at any time; and as I'm so deuced hard-up, it isn't likely we can be married yet awhile. But however dark I may want things kept just now, dear—though why they should be kept dark, I don't know—and yet, perhaps it is better; anyhow I mean to act fair and above-board with you, Dolly. I call you Dolly after Dolly Varden, you know,—an innkeeper's daughter, wasn't she? and in love with a blacksmith's son? I remember all about it. Yes, dear, I'm not a particularly good fellow; but I'll be good and true to you, so help me —"

This was quite an invitation to the plump little hand, which flew up to his lips like a fat little bird, and was kissed slyly before it went down again. Such conversations as this were carried on in furtive whispers during Mr. Dobb's Sunday-evening assemblies; and the lovers enjoyed each other's society in a corner of the little parlour, and were almost as much isolated in the magic world of their own creation as if the facetious clerk's imitations of Charles Kean and Paul Bedford had been the rustling of forest-leaves murmuring softly in the depths of some impenetrable silvan glade.

Mr. Dobb was a great deal too much interested in himself to be acutely conscious of other people's proceedings, and Selina favoured the lovers. She might perhaps be a little inclined to envy Dorothy her aristocratic conquest; but then the aristocrat was poor, and there seemed little chance of a six-roomed villa and a maid-of-all-work for the young couple yet awhile. Mrs. Dobb preached prudence; but she was rather gratified by the patrician flavour which Gervoise Catheron's presence imparted to her husband's receptions; and she was inclined to forgive Dorothy for being pretty; and even went so far as to admit that the bailiff's daughter was rather nice-looking; "though to my taste a pale complexion and regular features are much more interesting," said Mrs. Dobb, who had a thin face, which looked as if it had been carved out of yellow soap with a penknife, like those wonderful figures which the French painter Prudhon modelled in his inspired boyhood.

Dorothy was happy. Marcia Denison, hearing her little favourite's tripping foot, and watching the varying sunshine in her fresh young face, thought half-wonderingly what a beautiful thing youth was when it could be so bright, even without love. Sometimes, when the evidence of the girl's happiness broke out in some little burst of girlish gaiety, Miss Denison's thoughts shaped themselves into the words of Alfred de Musset, and she would fain have asked her little maid the poet's question:

> "Ninon, Ninon, que fais-tu de la vie?
> . . . . . .
> Comment vis-tu, toi qui n'as pas d'amour?"

Sometimes she talked to Dorothy of her father's house and her blacksmith cousins, half thinking that there must be some rustic lover lurking in the background, and that a few words of encouragement would win the secret from the petted little *protégée*. But the bailiff's daughter spoke of her cousins and her home-acquaintance with a careless freedom that was quite incompatible with the existence of any thing like a tender secret in that direction; and Marcia knew nothing of Mr. Dobb's evening-parties, for Dorothy had shrunk from telling her mistress of those beer-drinking assemblies which must have seemed such vulgar orgies to Sir Jasper's daughter. So Marcia was fain to believe that it was the brightness of youth, and youth only, that beamed in Dorothy's face.

"It is only when one feels youth gliding away that it seems a sad thing not to be loved," thought Marcia; who, with her twenty-fourth birthday stealing towards her, felt herself terribly old. She looked at herself sometimes in the glass. No, there were no wrinkles in the pale still face, the dark-gray eyes were clear and luminous; but oh, what a cold light it seemed that sparkled in them, when compared with the sunshine for ever playing in Dorothy's hazel orbs! what a look of settled sadness was spread like a dusky veil over the face that Marcia beheld when she turned from the contemplation of her joyous little maid to the contemplation of herself! "Is it any wonder there is a difference between us?" she thought; "her father loves her, and she has brothers and sisters and cousins; while I am quite alone. I can see a picture of my father sometimes as he would look at me if I were dead. 'Poor Marcia, poor girl,' he would say; 'and one finishes by being like that!—very sad, very unpleasant;' and then he would shrug his shoulders and stroll away, muttering some quotation from Voltaire or Holbach or Condorcet. Ah, papa, if you had only loved me, I think I could have won you away from Voltaire."

She clasped her hands involuntarily, and sudden tears sprang up to her eyes, for the random thought brought before her such a vivid vision of what might have been,—a father lured away from the dry logic-chopping of the Encyclopédists to listen to the simplest words that ever clothed sublime thoughts in common language.

CHAPTER II.

THE WIDOW TEARS HERSELF AWAY.

MARCIA DENISON had never felt more completely alone than she did during the winter months in which the lively widow condescended to waste her splendour on the desert air of Scarsdale Abbey. Whatever fragile ties of companionship there had been between herself and her father had made themselves air and vanished before the advent of Sir Jasper's brilliant visitor. Mrs. Harding could play *écarté* infinitely better than Marcia; so the Baronet and his daughter no longer spent a nightly hour at the tiny card-table, by the specially luxurious chair which was reserved in each apartment for the master of the Abbey. Marcia's dreamy little songs had been wont to soothe her father to his placid evening slumber; for there was no time of day or evening which the Baronet did not think profitably employed in a luxurious nap. But he no longer cared to hear "Break, break, break," or "Soft and low," or that tenderest and sweetest song that was ever composed by earthly poet, that plaintive ballad of Longfellow's, in whose mournful music we hear the ripple of the quiet tide as it creeps in and out among the wooden piles, and the solemn booming of the church-bell chiming midnight. Sir Jasper had rather liked these pensive ballads when he and Marcia had dawdled through the long winter evenings in a pleasant idleness that afforded so much leisure for thought.

"That song of Longfellow's always makes me cry," said the Baronet. "I don't know why we should be lachrymose because some fellow stood on a bridge at midnight when the clocks were striking the hour. I've done the same myself on Westminster Bridge after a debate, when I had the honour of representing my native county; but I wasn't sentimental. Westminster Abbey was close at hand; but the divine *afflatus* must have been a long way off, for I was not inspired.

We are a commercial people, Marcia, and I don't suppose we shall ever have another Shakespeare. Not that I regret the fact; for, taking into consideration the fuss we make about *one*, and the way in which we come to grief and insult one another every time we attempt to pay him any *post-mortem* civility, from the days of Garrick and Foote downwards, I should imagine that existence would be unendurable if we had *two*. Fortunately, it is not likely: the circumstances of the age are against another Williams. Your Shakespeare must begin by holding horses at the doors of a theatre; and as people don't generally go to the play on horseback nowadays, I can't see how he could get over that. The next best thing for him would be to burst from among the watermen who bawl for your carriage, and get in your way when you are stepping into it; but unless stupidity in the commonest matters is the sign of a lofty genius, I can't say I've ever met with an incipient bard amongst those gentlemen. No, my dear Marcia, we are a manufacturing people. You may depend upon it that poetry went out when tall chimneys came in. How can Westminster Abbey inspire a man nowadays? He surveys it with a shiver of horror at the idea of being buried in the neighbourhood of so much soap-boiling. And yet poetry is a very nice thing. That man Longfellow twists a few simple words about a meditative dawdler and a bridge, and the moon and the water and a church-clock, into the simplest rhyme; and lo! the hardest wretch who ever read mathematics cannot hear it sung without a choking sensation in his throat and a mist before his eyes. Arrange the words any other way, and they are dull and meaningless; alter a syllable, and the magical music is broken into discord. So the notes that make 'Hope told a flattering tale' only want the twist of a clever plagiarist to transform them into a comic Ethiopian melody; and the 'Old English Gentleman' is only the 'Last rose of summer' in disguise. So it is, after all, the arrangement that makes the genius. One man finds some celery-plants that have outgrown their basket, and we have the crowning glory of Corinthian architecture; another man looks up and sees the overarching branches in a forest-avenue, and all the cities of the earth are beautified by Gothic temples. And you and I will sit still and enjoy ourselves, my dear, happily conscious that every day a hundred aching brains are racking themselves to find out something for our advantage,—from the amiable philanthropist who devotes his attention to our kitchen-stoves, to the monomaniac who tries to find us the philosopher's stone."

Miss Denison had been very well contented to spend the long evenings and dusky winter afternoons in her father's society. A pleasant familiarity—respectful on her side, cordial on his—had existed between them. The Baronet, who had overlooked his daughter during her sister's lifetime, resigned himself to his destiny now that he found himself thrown upon her for society. He treated her very much as he might have treated any agreeable young lady whom circumstances rendered an inmate of his house; and Marcia had been one of the most patient companions who ever made a lonely man's home delightful. She had been his antagonist at *écarté*, and had sung her pensive ballads, and played her dreamy nocturnes and classic sonatas, her sleepy murmurings of summer seas, whispering in minor arpeggios, her trickling rivulets and fountains, her dawns and twilights and monastic bells, and all the sentimental musings of modern composers, with an untiring desire to please her solitary companion. She had been the most attentive and unwearying of listeners when her father was pleased to air his frivolous fancies; an intelligent listener too, as the Baronet knew very well, though she rarely ventured to argue with him. In short, they had been almost happy together; and although she had never been loved by her father, Marcia Denison felt a sharp little twinge, that was almost a pang of jealousy, when the gorgeous widow usurped her place, and assumed the task of amusing Sir Jasper, who was by no means unamusable, and was indeed a very placable sultan, so long as he was allowed to enjoy himself after his own fashion.

But how was it that Mrs. Harding succeeded in pushing Marcia so completely aside, and constituting herself Sir Jasper's chief companion? How was it that the Baronet found Blanche Harding, the superficial and pretentious, a more agreeable companion than gentle Marcia, whose intelligence was so sweetly tempered by feminine modesty, whose manners were so exquisitely sympathetic and refined? Marcia, sitting silently on one side of the fireplace while Sir Jasper and Mrs. Harding played écarté and talked shallow nonsense on the other, was not slow to perceive whence the charm of the siren was derived. The widow drew her most potent magic from the vanity of her victim, and her highest art consisted in a skilful cultivation of his own weakness. She flattered him. Sir Jasper was mortal, and Sir Jasper liked incense. Mrs. Harding kept the perfumed censer burning as steadily as if it had been the sacred fire which classic vestals watched before the fall of Rhea and the birth of Rome. In every word, in every gesture, in every glance, in every tone, Blanche Harding contrived to convey some breath of the insidious vapour whose enervating influence lulled the Baronet into a delicious trance of self-complacency. The first effort of a clever woman, who wants to make a man madly in love with her, is to make him madly in love with himself. Mrs. Harding advanced very rapidly in this initiatory process; but she was looking out every day for the triumphant hour in which the Baronet should glide unconsciously from self-complacency into admiration,—the hour in which, instead of murmuring calmly, " Well, I really am a most irresistible fellow, and that is an extremely sensible person ;" he should exclaim, in a rapture of enthusiasm, " Her presence is the light of my soul, and without her life would be a burden!"

It was for this mystical transition that Mrs. Harding watched; but the magic moment was slow to come. Sir Jasper accepted the incense and invited the consumption of more, until, in a metaphorical sense, the widow's arm ached from perpetual swinging of the censer; but Sir Jasper evidently considered the hospitality of the Abbey sufficient recompense for all Blanche Harding's pretty flatteries, and had no idea of offering any better payment for her agreeable adulation. The crowning merit of a clever woman's flattery is the fact that it never seems like flattery; and the unbelieving Baronet accepted every syllable of Mrs. Harding's honeyed discourse, and was in no way conscious that she was any thing but a very sensible woman,—a little worldly-wise, of course, and quite capable of pouncing upon any chance of making herself Lady Denison, yet in a general way a really candid creature, with plenty of sound common-sense. And then, comparing her with his daughter, Sir Jasper found that she was such an enthusiastic and appreciative being. How delightful it was to see her dark eyes flash with a vivid light, and her splendid countenance brighten with a sudden glory that was almost supernal, as she warmed into enthusiasm with some discourse of her host's, exclaiming at its close, "Ah, Sir Jasper, you should have been an orator! I can imagine nothing since Edmund Burke's speech about Marie Antoinette equal to that little burst of eloquence of yours just now, and yet I'll wager you scarcely knew you were eloquent;" or, "Oh, Sir Jasper, if you had only been a barrister! My pet, Brougham, would have had to look to his laurels, I fear; and yet your style is scarcely Brougham's: there is a lightness, a playfulness, a *je ne sais quoi*, a—may I venture to use a slang word?—a *chic*, which is all your own. But I am only a stupid woman, and I daresay I am talking nonsense!" Mrs. Harding would cry, in conclusion, with childlike *naïveté;* but Sir Jasper was wondrously tolerant of this kind of nonsense.

And yet Mrs. Harding was not satisfied. Alone in her own room, she lingered over the brushing of her long black hair. There were tresses which she put away in boxes; but the growing locks were by no means scanty; for there are women who cannot keep their souls unsullied in the conflict of life, but who can yet preserve a handsome parting to their dying day. The people whose hair turns gray, or whose ringlets grow scanty from the tortures of remorse, are not many. Robespierre's bilious constitution had more influence upon his complexion than the blood of all the Girondists; and no doubt the dictator suffered a more terrible visitation in the way of nightmare from the jam-tarts which he stole in his youth than ever he did from the phantom of Madame Roland.

Mrs. Harding had done many bad things in her life, but she had been very careful of her complexion. She had never consumed the scholar's midnight-oil, or impaired her digestion by ill-chosen viands; and the finger of Care had written few lines upon her broad white forehead. The florid widow had been established at Scarsdale Abbey for nearly three months, and her face assumed rather an anxious expression when she looked at herself in the glass. It was the face of a woman who was scarcely likely to take the smallest step in life without a settled purpose, and it was growing day by day into the face of a woman who began to look gloomily forward to the possibility of failure. If Mrs. Harding were a coquette, bent only on demanding perpetual tribute of admiration, and had come to the Abbey with a view to the subjugation of Sir Jasper beneath the influence of her fascinations, surely she had every reason to be content with her success.

Mark Antony at his weakest never abandoned himself more completely to the sway of Cleopatra than the cynical Baronet to the charms of his guest. Night after night he basked in the light of her beauty, and was intoxicated by the conversational bon-bons which she so insidiously administered to him. But if, on the other hand, the brilliant widow had come to Scarsdale with more serious intentions,—if she wished to make herself mistress of the Baronet's hand and fortune,—she certainly had made no progress whatever, and had good reason to frown moodily at the unprofitable beauty which she contemplated nightly while busy with her hairbrushes.

Sir Jasper was fascinated; but he was cautious Sir Jasper kissed the yoke of the fair enslaver; but he knew how to take care of himself. When Mrs. Harding's flatteries were sweetest, when the intoxicating drop of intellectual noyeau, or golden water, or maraschino, in the conversational bonbon, was most delicious to the epicure's palate, prudence, for ever on the watch, prompted Sir Jasper's tongue. He accepted all the pretty attentions which made his evenings so pleasant; but he accepted them under a protest, so artfully conveyed as to be inoffensive. He was an old man, he said; he had arrived at an age when a man could bask in the sunshine of feminine loveliness without fear of fever or sun-stroke.

"For a man of my age, Venus, the implacable goddess, transforms herself into a nursing sister, and Cupid changes his venomous arrow into the spoon that stirs an invalid's messes of beef-tea and barley-water. A man of my age is not entirely a useless twaddler, for upon him lovely woman can practise and bring to perfection the arts by which she may hereafter subjugate her youthful adorers. It is only at my time of life, when love would be imbecility and marriage an act of dotage, that a man can derive unalloyed enjoyment from feminine society. He may be as eloquent as he pleases in praise of the loveliness that fascinates him, the wit that cheers his declining hours, the tenderness that compassionates his afflictions, and he has no fear that his unstudied phrases will be recited in a witness-box amidst the titter of a crowded court, or form the subject of flippant witticism from a popular Q.C."

Thus playfully the Baronet defended himself, even when the widow was most enchanting, and her victim's subjugation most complete. Sometimes Mrs. Harding talked of leaving the Abbey, and the Baronet expressed himself as disconsolate beyond measure at the idea of her departure. "What would Marcia do without her delightful friend!" he exclaimed; "and what would Marcia's papa do without his Spanish ballads and *écarté!*" Sir Jasper urged that he was a very old man; and that the whims of a very old man should meet with some indulgence from the hands of compassionate Beauty; even though compassionate Beauty was eager to spread her wings and soar to fairer scenes.

"I know that Scarsdale is a kind of modern moated grange," he said; "and that you must be very often aweary, aweary, and wish your dismal entertainers dead, even if you don't wish yourself in that disadvantageous position; but, if you can endure us a little longer, be merciful, and furl your wings at our hearth for a week or two before you flutter away to the other butterflies."

Of course Mrs. Harding protested that she had been unspeakably happy at the dear old Abbey. Every place she visited was 'dear' and 'old' in the widow's florid vocabulary. She had many engagements for the spring, and she had brought all kinds of disgrace upon herself, and had offended troops of friends by her lengthened stay at Scarsdale; but if dear Sir Jasper said she was to stay another week, she could not resist his flattering request, and she must go on offending people, and stay at any hazard.

This little business had been gone through four or five times, and the quaintly-cropped yew-trees in Marcia's old-fashioned garden were swaying to and fro in the shrill March winds, when Mrs. Harding found out, after many nights of moody contemplation in the glass, that she really could not prolong her delightful visit any further, for that a dear friend, residing in the neighbourhood of Maida Vale, whom she had promised to visit early in January, would not be put off any longer. "If my friend were not an invalid, I don't think I could tear myself away even now," the widow murmured, with a plaintive sigh; "but it is duty rather than pleasure that takes me away from you, dearest Marcia. You will not see my name in your *Post*, Sir Jasper, at any of the great parties of the season; I shall be sitting beside a sick couch, and dawdling away the quiet hours in a darkened room. My utmost gaiety will be an occasional drive round the Park. And oh, how I shall remember our happy evenings here, Marcia!" exclaimed the widow, seizing Miss Denison's listless hand, and vainly inviting that young lady to join her in a gush.

Marcia had not pressed the widow to remain, and did not utter any lamentations when her guest's departure grew imminent. She had never liked Mrs. Harding; she had liked her less from the day on which the widow had expressed herself in vague denunciation of George Pauncefort. There were times when Miss Denison had occasion to struggle with an uncomfortable feeling about this brilliant widow,—a feeling which was very much like detestation.

"I shall be a better Christian when she is gone," thought Marcia. "How is it that papa can accept her odious flatteries, and not perceive how false and hollow she is? He cannot believe St. Matthew, and yet he will take every word of this horrible woman's for gospel truth."

When once Mrs. Harding had announced that her invalid friend in Maida Vale could wait no longer, she lost no time in putting her threat of departure into execution. She talked of her departure during breakfast; announced after breakfast that she was going to devote the day to the packing of her trunks, in order to leave Searsdale early on the morrow. She watched Sir Jasper rather closely as she talked of this packing business; but the Baronet did not flinch. He offered her the services of his daughter's maid, and begged her to consider his entire household at her disposal.

"In this instance it is an act of sublime abnegation to speed the parting guest," said Sir Jasper; "but since you are bent on leaving us, we are bound to smooth the way for your comfortable departure. When you are tired of the gay world—ah, I forgot; an invalid lady, to be sure," murmured the Baronet, as Mrs. Harding was about to interrupt him. "When you have tried another species of moated grange, you may be resigned to the idea of coming back to us; in the early autumn, perhaps, when every break in the wood is a Creswick, and every corn-field a Linnell. Come to us in the autumn, if you can. You won't be able to stand your invalid friend very long, depend upon it. The brightest spirit will droop in a perpetual atmosphere of beef-tea; and there will be time for a round of visits between this and the autumn. You can pay off all your debts, or at any rate make a composition with your creditors, at the rate of a week in the month, say; and you can return to us when the reapers are reaping early in among the bearded barley, which doesn't rhyme with early, by the by, any more than Oliver Goldsmith's 'kay' rhymed with 'be.' Yes, let us hope you will come back to us; let us hope it, even if you don't come. If Adam and Eve had been allowed to anticipate a possible return to Eden, half the bitterness of that first great ejectment would have been taken away."

When the Baronet retired to his favourite retreat under the shadow of Neptune, Mrs. Harding went to her rooms, and began the grand process of packing those glistening moires and lustrous velvets which had gratified her host's feeling for colour during the winter evenings, as well as the pretty cashmeres and foulards in which she had burst brightly upon him every morning, in a carefully-studied dishabille. The widow's brow was very moody while she folded all these trappings of feminine warfare, and put away a perfect arsenal of delicate implements by which she was wont to effect the decorative portion of her toilet. More than once in the process of her packing Mrs. Harding happened to find herself in need of masculine assistance. She wanted *Times* Supplements to lay at the top of her boxes; and with Sir Jasper's entire household at her disposal, she preferred to appeal to Sir Jasper himself. She invaded the Baronet's retreat with many apologies, and a great deal of ceremony; and while Sir Jasper abandoned the perusal of Mr. Newman's *Phases of Faith* to hunt obscure shelves for old newspapers, she wandered into gushing lamentations about the necessity of departure. But the Baronet's prudence did not desert him even in this trying moment, and he handed her the Supplements as coolly as if he were selling waste-paper to a Roxborough butterman.

"How kind you are! and how I shall miss you, Sir Jasper!" murmured the widow sadly; "and what a lost creature I shall seem when I have no longer your powerful intellect to help me whenever I am at a loss!" Mrs. Harding's manner might have implied that the *Times* Supplements just handed her by the Baronet involved a service which nobody else upon earth could have performed for her. "And yet," she added, looking at the Baronet contemplatively, in her pet attitude, and breathing a profound sigh, "perhaps it's a very good thing I am going away, for I have felt my opinions growing terribly unsettled lately; and heaven only knows what would have become of me, morally speaking, if I had stayed much longer. Do you remember what Coventry Patmore says? 'Take heed what his religion is, for yours ere long will be the same.' That was said to a woman about the man whom she was going to marry; but what can be stronger than the influence of a friend whom we respect and admire?" The widow dropped her voice at the last words, and executed a little manœuvre with her eyelashes, which was the next best thing to blushing. "Yes, Sir Jasper," she continued, in her most pensive tone, "I am glad I am going; you have been a dangerous companion for me."

The Baronet simpered. The weakest side of his character was undergoing a sharp attack. Mrs. Harding was something like the warrior king who thought that Paris was worth a mass, and would have written herself down a Voltairean without a moment's hesitation, if by that small sacrifice she might have attained any tangible advantage. The bon-bon was peculiarly seductive; but even in swallowing it, the Baronet was strong.

"You undervalue your own force of intellect, my dear Mrs. Harding," he said; "your mind is

THE WIDOW TEARS HERSELF AWAY. 43

too powerful to be influenced by mine. It is I who have occasion to fear you. At present I believe nothing, and am resigned. If I listened to you, I should believe a little and—be miserable."

Throughout that day Sir Jasper was fluttered in his retirement by the incursions of the brilliant widow. She wanted adhesive labels for her trunks, and she imagined the Baronet's study the place of all places in which to find them. She wanted to know all about the trains; and Sir Jasper was the only person whose intellect could cope with the Rhadamanthine Bradshaw. And on every visit to the library there was a little conversation—now pensive, now playful. But when Mrs. Harding had concluded her packing and dressed for dinner, her face was still clouded, and there was a hard dissatisfied expression about her mouth which argued ill for the result of her long visit.

She dressed herself in the dark silk in which she intended to travel next day. It was only four o'clock when her toilet was completed, and she stood looking out of her window in a listless attitude, with a countenance which was very different from the bright face that had so lately beamed upon Sir Jasper Denison.

"Would it be so very high a prize, after all, to be mistress of so many trees and so much grass," she thought, "and to hold a certain rank among a few stuck-up country families? The Catherons were greater people, once upon a time, than any family within twenty miles of Roxborough; but I dare not own to the name of Catheron."

It was a fine bright afternoon, and the rooks were rejoicing noisily in the chill sunshine. After standing some time in gloomy contemplation of the landscape, Mrs. Harding turned impatiently away from the window.

"I'll go out," she muttered; "perhaps a little rapid walking in the fresh air will put me in a better temper."

She wrapt herself in a large velvet mantle with loose sleeves that enveloped her bare arms to the wrist, and she put on a Spanish hat and feather which were infinitely becoming to her bold beauty. She had seen nothing of Marcia all that day; and even now she did not seek Miss Denison, but went straight to a little door leading out upon the terrace, and walked across the broad lawn and the great deer-park, and far away into the woods.

Something—scarcely a definite purpose, but rather an irresistible fascination—led the widow towards the romantic spot in which Mr. Pauncefort's habitation was hidden. She walked briskly along the narrow winding path, with the wind blowing round her, and her velvet mantle wrapped closely about her; but within a hundred yards of the Hermitage, at a point where two pathways diverged into the depth of the woodland, she stopped suddenly, arrested by the sight of a little group in the distance.

It was a group of three figures—Marcia, Mr. Pauncefort, and Dorothy Tursgood, whose bright scarlet cloak and basket made her look like a bouncing Red Ridinghood. Mrs Harding drew aside into the shadow of the trees and watched the distant figures. Sir Jasper's tenant and Sir Jasper's daughter were in the act of shaking hands, while Dorothy stood meekly by.

"Very cordial indeed, Miss Denison," muttered

the widow spitefully. "I understand now why you and I cannot get on together. I am disliked because I am no friend of Mr. Pauncefort." Then after a pause the watcher thought, "Has he told her any thing? No; he is too proud to speak. He would perish with his secret untold. I have reason to know how much he will suffer for the gratification of his pride

George Pauncefort and Marcia lingered for a few minutes after they had shaken hands. The tenant of the Hermitage had accompanied Miss Denison in one of her charitable missions to the village. They loitered talking, and the two voices rang out upon the evening air, the man's deep and sonorous, the woman's very clear and sweet; and then George Pauncefort lifted his hat, little Dorothy dropped a curtsey, and Marcia and her attendant walked away briskly by a pathway that branched off in the direction of the Abbey.

By keeping straight on, Mrs. Harding must come face to face with Sir Jasper's tenant. She kept straight on, watching the countenance of the man who was walking towards her without seeing her. The tenant's face had been very bright as he parted from Marcia, but it darkened little by little as he came nearer to the widow; and when he looked up suddenly, startled by the rustling of her silken garments, it was the face of a man who has very little to hope for on this earth. It darkened still more as he recognised Mrs. Harding. "You!" he muttered, and then bowing stiffly, would have walked on.

The widow stopped him. There was a reckless audacity in her manner of looking at him, in the tone of her voice when she spoke to him, that was almost like the insolence of some demoniac creature defying the superior being who has trampled upon it.

"A meeting with me is very unwelcome just now, I daresay, Mr. —— Pauncefort," she said sneeringly. The little pause she made before addressing him by the name he bore at Searsdale told as plainly as the plainest words that Pauncefort was not his real name, and that his real name was known to her.

"A meeting with you any where, under any

circumstances, must always be unwelcome to me," answered Sir Jasper's tenant, still trying to pass the widow, and with his passage still barred by her portly figure and spreading draperies.

"But peculiarly unwelcome this afternoon, I know," she said.

"Peculiarly unwelcome this afternoon. Too strong a contrast is always unpleasant."

"And the contrast between Marcia Denison and me is very strong, I suppose."

"Thank God, yes!"

"What reason have you to be thankful about her?" cried the widow; "she is nothing to you, and never can be any thing to you."

"She is a great deal to me. She is the woman who, when my respect for womanhood had perished altogether, as I thought, taught me that womanhood can still be beautiful. She has taught me that a woman can be charming, and yet not a hypocrite; handsome, and not a shallow coquette. She has taught me the possibility of happy husbands, secure in the love of faithful wives; of mothers who do not desert their sick children; of sisters in whose girlish confidences the devil has no reason to rejoice. Caroline!" cried George Pauncefort suddenly, "why do you force yourself upon me; I have spent the best years of my lifetime among the wildest and dreariest regions that civilised man ever penetrated, in the vain hope that I might forget your face, and the time when it was familiar to me. I come back, worn in health, broken in spirit, to find some little spot where I might rest forgotten under the shadow of English foliage, within the reach of English faces to watch me when I am dying,—and even here, in this one corner of the earth, where I am resigned to live and die, alike forgotten by all who know me or my kindred,—even here you pursue me; even here the bitterest memories of my life are revived more vividly than ever by the sight of your face. Have I ever done you any unkindness, or denied you any privilege?"

"Oh, no," answered Mrs. Harding, in the same sneering tone which she had used before;

"you have been very generous—with the money which you do not want. If you have spared those who injured you, you have spared them for the gratification of your own pride, not out of mercy for them. I do not think there is any cause for gratitude on my part."

"Perhaps not," answered the tenant sadly; "I have spared my pride: and I have spared my name. *That* has not been dragged in the dust. Now let me pass. I shall leave this place tomorrow; I will not run the risk of meeting you again."

"There will be no danger of your doing so; I am going away myself early to-morrow. You need not leave your favourite retreat; you need not desert your new friends; you may still fetch and carry groceries and distribute tracts for the Dorcas Society—and Miss Denison."

"How dare you mention her name with a sneer!"

"How can I help sneering at the sentimental parting I witnessed just now?"

"Caroline," cried George Pauncefort, "I did

not think that even fifteen years' liberty to do wrong could transform you into such a demon!"

The widow's right arm was hanging loosely by her side; and, before she had time to resist him, Sir Jasper's tenant seized her wrist and flung the wide velvet sleeve back from the bare white arm, across which the scar was visible, unconcealed by band or bracelet. He held her arm for a moment, looking at it, and then let it drop.

"Forgive me," he said; "I began to think I was the victim of some hellish conspiracy. And now, if you have any thing to say to me, speak quickly, and let me go."

"I have nothing to say, except that I am going to London, and shall call on Mr. Williams, or write to him."

"He will be as well prepared to see you or hear from you as he has always been. Good afternoon."

"Good afternoon."

Once more Sir Jasper's tenant raised his hat,

more frigidly respectful in his gesture than when he had saluted Miss Denison. The widow watched him as he walked away. Then she looked at her watch, and, finding it long past six, hurried back to the Abbey.

CHAPTER III.

DID HE LOVE HER?

WHEN the widow had departed, a pleasant calm descended upon Marcia Denison's life. Once more she was her father's chief companion in the lonely evenings. The Baronet was, in a general way, resigned to every thing that could possibly happen to him, except physical pain or personal inconvenience, and he did not give utterance to any lamentations upon the loss of his brilliant visitor.

"I shall enjoy my Ettys more now that she is gone," the Baronet murmured complacently, as he settled himself in the yellow drawing-room after dining tête-à-tête with his daughter. "Those gaudy dresses of hers were the death of my pictures, and her flesh latterly has not been up to the mark. There has been a woolliness about her cheeks, and a want of feeling in her chin, which considerably deteriorated my enjoyment of her society. There is more truth in your mezzotints, my dear Marcia; and that ivory whiteness of yours, if produced by art, would be a miracle. Your eyes are not quite up to the Greuze standard, but they are very fine, and the modelling of the eyelids is really charming."

The widow's back once fairly turned, the treacherous Baronet lost no time in writing to his tenant.

"Dear Pauncefort," wrote the traitor,—"she is gone. I found it impossible to hasten her departure without *esclandre*, so allowed her to take her own time about it. I'm sorry you don't approve of her antecedents, for she is really a very agreeable woman. Marcia and she have not hit it very well together, and there has been a kind of tacit avoidance of each other on the part of both women, though I did not communicate the contents of your letter to my daughter.

"Come and see me. I languish for a little vigorous conversation upon subjects that are worth talking about, if there is any thing in the world really worth talking about. I am enervated by the perpetual society of women, and am weary to sickness of my own thoughts. Come, dear Pauncefort; you will find your old place waiting for you, and two stupid people brightened by your coming.

"Always yours,
"Jasper Denison."

"I don't believe he is a scoundrel, whatever the widow may say," thought the Baronet, as he folded and sealed his letter. "She is prejudiced, I daresay. Met him in early life perhaps, when he was better off, and laid siege to him with a view to matrimonial arrangements, and found him cautious. A widow never forgives a man for being cautious; and although I don't know when the estimable Harding departed this life,

I should think, from the perfection to which the brilliant Blanche has brought her art, that she has been a widow for a long time,—indeed, if such a thing were practicable, I should be inclined to believe she had been born a widow. However, I'll talk to Pauncefort about her."

Sir Jasper's tenant answered the friendly letter in as friendly a tone: but he was by no means prompt in his acceptance of his landlord's invitation. For a long time — all through the month of April and far into the month of May — Marcia saw nothing of the African traveller in her afternoon walks. He was away, Dorothy told her,—away on a pedestrian excursion, with a knapsack on his shoulder, and the mongrel cur for his sole companion. And Miss Denison, passing by the break in the wood where she had so often met him, was fain to confess to herself that she missed him very much, and that her woodland rambles seemed very dreary without him.

"My life has been so friendless and empty, that it is scarcely strange that I should cling to this one friend," she thought, sadly.

And then, having once made for herself a valid excuse for giving George Pauncefort such an important place in her thoughts, Marcia found herself thinking of him very frequently. In all her life he had borne part. She had no favourite books whose choicer passages had not been freely discussed in the long autumnal evenings, or the winter walks between the Park and the village: she had no music that was not more or less associated with him, and his keen appreciation of all that was grandest and highest in it. To her father, the trickling arpeggios and treble tremulos of a modern nocturne were all-sufficient: but George Pauncefort had a higher taste, and a keener sense of all that is grandest in music: and for his gratification she had searched for dusty volumes of the classic composers, and had been content to practise sedulously in the morning, in order that she might delight her father's guest in the evening. In art, as in music, she had found his taste of a higher order than Sir Jasper's, and they had sided together against the Baronet in many a pleasant argument about Vandervelde and Bakhuysen, Reynolds and Romney, Cuyp and Potter, Watteau and Laucret, and all the great painters of the past and present. In so narrow a circle as Marcia Denison's, a figure once admitted must needs become a very prominent one: and it was only when George Pauncefort had departed on his vagabond wanderings that she discovered how very much he had been to her.

"Why is he so capricious and fitful in his intercourse with us?" she thought. "He likes us; there can be no doubt of that; for I am sure he is the last man in the world to affect a friendship which he does not feel. And we have been so intimate: a friend of twenty years' standing could scarcely seem more thoroughly at home by our fireside than he has done. And yet all at once he goes away, and we neither hear nor see any thing of him for months together."

It was not quite two months yet since Miss Denison had met George Pauncefort on her way to the village, but it seemed so long. Thinking over his conduct very often,—thinking of many things which cannot be shaped into common words, or yet transcribed upon this common page, — thinking of chance accents in his voice, of glances so brief that it was almost difficult to decide whether they had really been, or had only been imagined by herself,—thinking of him more constantly than she was aware, Marcia could only come to one conclusion about him: he liked her— very much—he—!

Sitting by herself in the May sunshine, looking pensively out at the Park, a crimson flush flew over Marcia's face, like the reflection of a glowing sunset, as she shaped this unfinished thought. Was it not something more than friendly liking which she had seen in George Pauncefort's face sometimes when they parted in the wood? How the still evening hour came back to her; with the faint pressure of his hand; the low glinting light between the trunks of the trees; the distant cawing of the rooks! How it all came back to her, and what a tender sweetness there was in the recollection,—a rapture deeper than any joy she had ever known before,—a tumultuous delight that carried her away from the common earth!

She clasped her hands before her face to hide those crimson blushes.

"And this is what happiness is like!" she thought. "I do not wonder that it comes only once in a lifetime,—in some sad lives not at all."

And then, seized with a sudden terror, she asked herself, "Is it true,—is it really true? Can it be true that some one loves me at last?"

The doubt lasted only a moment. We may mistake paste for a diamond, or a copy for a Rembrandt: but we can never mistake a diamond for paste, or a Rembrandt for a copy. So with love: the worthless tinsel may sometimes seem like gold: the pure gold can never seem like tinsel. Inexperienced as Marcia was, she knew that George Pauncefort loved her, and that some powerful motive kept him silent.

"He is poor, and I am rich," she thought; "that is the secret of his capricious conduct. He will sacrifice his happiness to his pride, and he will never speak. I know now how proud he is; for I can remember his face that day when he spoke of his native county,—the neglected garden of his old home. Ah, what happiness if my worthless money could restore the place he loves, and build up the name that has fallen!"

Like most people who have never known what it is to want money, Marcia Denison was very apt to undervalue that useful commodity: but when she thought of what her fortune might do for George Pauncefort, she began to fancy that it was a grand thing to be rich, after all.

But would he ever accept her money? would he ever give her the opportunity of helping him to regain his lost position? He had been away nearly two months: and Dorothy, who was always well informed about affairs at the Hermitage, told her mistress that Mr. Pauncefort's man did not know where his master was, or when he might be expected home.

"And oh, Miss Marcia," exclaimed Dorothy, in conclusion, "when I went to see my grandmother the other night, Mr. Milward was in the kitchen, and talking about his master's being away so long. He said it gave him the horrors sometimes to think of Mr. Pauncefort tramping, and tramping, and tramping quite alone among the wildest and most solitary places, very often long after dark, and in all kinds of dreadful weather; and sometimes, Mr. Milward said, he felt almost afraid to take up the newspaper, for fear he should read the account of a body found somewhere, washed away by a rising tide, or killed by a fall from a crag, or smothered in the mud of some horrible marsh. But oh, Miss Marcia, how pale you look!" cried Dorothy; "and how silly of me to talk about these dreadful things!"

Marcia blushed, ashamed of having betrayed so much emotion, even before the eyes of guileless Dorothy; but though the little maid was so deeply in love herself, she did not recognise the tokens of the tender passion in her dignified young mistress. To Dorothy's mind Mr. Pauncefort was a very elderly person, for whom it was impossible to entertain any warmer feeling than a respectful compassion. But upon Marcia this speech of Dorothy's had a profound effect. Her imagination—a hundred times more vivid than the imagination of the valet—seized upon the faint sketch suggested by him, and filled-in all the details of a horrible picture, which haunted her sleeping or waking.

From that hour there was no change in the sky which Marcia Denison did not think of with reference to the lonely wanderer far away among careless strangers, with no better friend than a ragamuffin dog. There was no dark night under whose starless canopy she did not fancy him, alone upon a dangerous track, careless of the perils that hemmed him in,—reckless of the life that gave him so little happiness. Sometimes, standing at an open window, long after the quiet household had been hushed in sleep, she was carried away by the vividness of her fancies, and saw him battling against the driving wind upon some craggy mountain-slope, as distinctly as if the woodland landscape had been reft asunder and that other scene revealed beyond. Sometimes, subdued completely beneath the dominion of this thought, she would stretch her arms towards the distant figure, with a gesture full of imploring love, and cry aloud,—

"Oh, come back to me, come back to me! Why is your pride so cruel? Why do we both suffer so much useless misery?"

From the moment in which she had first confessed to herself that she was beloved, there had been no shadow of doubt in her mind. She knew that he loved her, and that it was love for her which had driven him away from his peaceful shelter. Humble though her estimate of her own merits, her own charms, she never paused to ask herself whether she was worthy of this man's love. It was no question for reasoning. It had come to her as the rain comes to the flowers. Revealed to her by a thousand evidences in themselves too small to be remembered, she scarcely could have told how she had discovered the delicious secret. She knew that he loved her; but she did not know why she knew it, and was content to believe that of which she had no better proof than her own conviction.

May melted into June, and Marcia thought "he will come back in June." But the last flowers upon the hawthorn bushes withered; the dog-roses unfolded their opal leaves; it was midsummer, and still he had not returned. Sir Jasper grumbled sorely at having no one but his daughter to talk to, and yet steadily set his face against any communication with the outraged country gentry, who did not recognise the Baronet's right to nurse his grief or indulge his eccentricity when the duties of society demanded that he should give dinner-parties. Dorothy told her mistress that Mr. Pauncefort's valet was getting really alarmed; and Marcia's heart sank with the tidings. These unsentimental people rarely are frightened unless there is serious cause for fear; and the thought of the man-servant's uneasiness had a terrible influence upon Marcia. When she went out alone now, her footsteps led her almost involuntarily towards that entrance to the wood which was nearest the Hermitage, and by which it was likely Mr. Pauncefort would return, if he ever returned. Yes, it had come to that now. It was an open question whether he would ever come back — whether the dark face would ever look down at her again; with unspeakable affection instinct in its every look; with so many transitions of expression, but with not one that was not tempered by love for her.

"Oh, come back to me, come back to me!" cried her heart, as she wandered alone in the shadowy pathways, where the wild-roses bloomed unheeded. "Come back to me!" cried her heart every day and every hour, as her lips cried sometimes in the dead night when there was none to hear her. Her love strengthened with every hour of his absence; for there is no love so profound as that which is developed in an atmosphere of terror. She thought of him so often now as of something that was lost to her—the only friend of her life, who by a dismal fatality had been taken away from her in the hour when first she knew how much she was beloved. "It is my fate," she thought sometimes; "I have never known what it is to be precious to any living creature; and now the one friend who would have cherished me is taken away." Her silent sorrow was very bitter; but she was accustomed to suffer and make no sign. Her fingers never touched the keys of her piano without the memory of *his* delight in certain passages of her music coming back to her like a sharp pain ; she never sang one of her simple ballads without recalling how *he* had been moved by their plaintive tenderness. And yet she sang and played to her father every evening; and the Baronet never divined that it was a mental anguish, and not a physical languor, under the influence of which his daughter drooped and grew paler day by day.

The family medical man was sent for, and administered tonics ; but no tonics could shut from her mind the picture of that lonely wanderer with whom her heart went forth into the dreary night; and Sir Jasper began to be concerned, in a gentlemanly way, for his only daughter's health.

June warmed into July, and storm-laden clouds hung heavily over the woody glades and hollows of Scarsdale. For a week Dorothy had paid no dutiful visit to the deaf old housekeeper at the Hermitage, and for a week Marcia had received no tidings of her father's tenant. She shrank with a proud reserve from making any inquiry about him, and endured the new anguish of suspense as bravely and as quietly as she had borne all the sorrows of her loveless girlhood.

She wandered from the Park to the wood in the still, oppressive afternoon. She had left the house with no settled purpose, but only because the quiet of her room had become intolerable to her. She was quite free to wander where she pleased; for Sir Jasper beguiled a considerable portion of his time in placid slumber during this threatening weather.

"I know that a storm is coming, and shall do my best to dodge it," said the Baronet. "If I can doze in my arm-chair, serenely unconscious of the avenging elements, the avenging elements may have their fling. I daresay they will take it out of my oaks, or my haymakers. The sleeper is an unassailable being who may defy creation. An earthquake can scarcely affect him; he will only awake somewhere else."

The storm-clouds had brooded so long above the woods that people had grown careless of the expected tempest, and Marcia wandered deep into the wood without any thought of danger. She had penetrated beyond the neighbourhood of the Hermitage into a shadowy glade, where the fern grew wild and high, and where the spreading branches made a dense roof of foliage that shut out the leaden sky. It was a spot in which she had spent many lonely summer afternoons long ago in her childhood, with a book for her companion, and a big shaggy dog for her protector. It was a spot into whose solemn depths she had not penetrated since her return from the Continent; and the memory of her solitary childhood came sharply back to her as she entered the familiar glade.

"In all the world there is no face but his which I have ever seen look brighter for the love of me," she thought, remembering her father's profound indifference, her sister's caressing patronage, and even little Dorothy's grateful affection, which was at best too much like the frisky fidelity of a frivolous lap-dog to supply the void in a lonely woman's heart. "In all the world there is no voice but his that ever trembled as it spoke to me. Shall I ever see his face or hear his voice again?"

She stopped suddenly; for close beside her path—almost at her feet—there lay the figure of a man half-buried among the broken fern, lying face downward, with his head resting on his folded arms.

Dorothy would have recognised the shabby shooting-coat, the dark tumbled hair. Marcia knew by some instinct which took no aid from sight that it was George Paunccfort who was lying at her feet. Her heart grew cold as she looked at the quiet figure. Alive—or dead, he was found.

But in a moment he had sprung to his feet, erect, and with his hands outstretched to meet hers. Her faint cry of surprise had startled him like a discharge of artillery close at his elbow. She gave him her hands freely, and suffered them to rest in his strong grasp. In her deep delight at seeing him once more, she forgot that no word had passed between them to make them any more than common friends. She almost forgot that they were any thing except affianced lovers, she had thought of him so much, and she knew so well that he loved her. If her belief in his affection had needed any confirmation, the light in his pale thin face as he looked at her might have confirmed it. She saw the supernal radiance, and had time to think about it while George Paunccfort held her hands in his, too deeply moved for speech.

"And papa can doubt in the divinity of a God," she thought, "when human affection has only to be tolerably free from the leaven of human selfishness in order to become almost divine."

Marcia was the first to speak.

"I began to think you were never coming back to us." (Ah, how sweet those two common words "to us" sounded from her lips: almost like the promise of a home!) "I am so glad to see you!"

"And I am so glad you are glad."

He released her hands, and they strolled onwards side by side, with the fern rustling round them as they walked along the narrow trackway that had been trodden through it. Marcia made no attempt to conceal her pleasure in this meeting; there were so many reasons for her frankness; and not the least among them was the shabby coat, which, with something of Dorothy's simplicity, Miss Denison accepted as the outward and visible sign of George Paunecfort's poverty. He was poor, and his youth was gone. He was not a man to be inflated into foppish pomposity by the evidence of a woman's friendship: and then she believed in him so implicitly.

While they were walking slowly side by side —silent for the moment, for there are joys too deep for eloquence—a distant peal of thunder startled them from their thoughtful silence.

"It is coming," cried Sir Jasper's tenant; "I have been expecting this storm for the last four days. You must hurry home, Miss Denison; or else—but I daresay there will be time for you to get home. Will you take my arm? we shall get along better so. Can you walk fast?"

"As fast as you please."

They hurried to the opening in the wood by which Marcia had diverged from the beaten path. Vivid flashes of lightning shot in upon them from between the foliage overhead; and the rattling thunder-peals seemed to shake the ground beneath their hastening feet. As they emerged from the glade into the pathway, there was a sudden pattering upon the leaves, and the rain came down as it does come sometimes in a thunder-storm, to the terror of farmers whose hay is not carried, or whose stacks are unthatched.

They were within a quarter of a mile of the Hermitage, and the Abbey was two miles off; so there could be little question as to the refuge which Marcia must seek from the torrents that were beating down the leaves and flooding the underwood.

"You can take shelter in my cottage," said Mr. Pauncefort, "and I will send my servant to the Abbey for the carriage. It is quite impossible for you to go home on foot in this weather."

Marcia assented without hesitation; and in ten minutes more she was safely sheltered in the old-fashioned parlour where Sir Jasper's tenant spent so much of his cheerless life. Dame Tursgood, summoned from the back premises with some difficulty, removed the young lady's dripping mantle, and made a hasty fire on the broad hearth. When he had seen this done, and Miss Denison seated comfortably in the big easy-chair by the fire, with her hat off, and her loosened hair hanging about her shoulders as wet as a naiad's, Mr. Pauncefort went away to despatch a messenger to the Abbey. He paused for a moment in the little stone passage before calling his servant.

"Shall I go myself?" he thought. "It would be better, perhaps; and a wet walk would not hurt *me*."

But Sir Jasper's tenant did not go himself. He despatched his servant, and then went slowly back to the parlour. What wonderful influence upon a man's destiny these small questions have sometimes!

He went back to the woman who loved him: he went back to his fate.

CHAPTER IV.

MISS DENISON'S HUMILIATION.

SIR JASPER's tenant went slowly back to the dusky chamber where Marcia was sitting, with the yellow light from the newly-kindled logs shining upon her. The light shone upon a pale thoughtful face; a very sad face, as it turned towards George Pauncefort.

The low old-fashioned parlour, usually as perfect as a Dutch picture in the order of its quaint arrangement, to-day wore a strange aspect. Open packing-cases yawned wide at one end of the room, and the centre table was piled high with books that had been taken from the worm-eaten oaken shelves; a few wonderful, but rather dingy-looking, engravings by Albert Durer had been removed from the walls, and were piled on one of the smaller tables. Only thus could look the room of a man who was about to remove his treasures.

"Is he going to sell his books and pictures?" wondered Marcia; and then her face grew paler, as she thought, "Perhaps he is going away."

The idea set her heart beating tumultuously; it had been such an irregularly-disposed heart lately. Going away! There was blank despair in the very thought. And yet an hour or two before, when she had fancied him dead and buried in some obscure resting-place, amongst people who had never known his name, she would have considered it happiness to be told that he was alive and well in the remotest valley that ever was sheltered by the shadow of the Himalayas.

She, who was so reserved towards every one else, had little reserve where he was concerned. She trusted him as she had never trusted any one upon earth; she believed in him as a man whose truth and goodness were only less infallible than the truth and goodness of Heaven.

"You are going to leave Scarsdale, Mr.

Pauncefort?" she said, as he closed the door behind him.

"Yes, Miss Denison," he answered sadly.

He did not go towards the hearth where she was seated, though the yellow light of the logs made that one spot bright and cheery. A grayish darkness brooded ominously outside the latticed casement; rich brown shadows filled the paneled room, making a picture for a modern Rembrandt, if there existed such a person; with heaven's own cloud and sunshine melted into liquid colour, and always ready for his brush.

George Pauncefort did not approach his guest, though the homelike aspect of that little bit of the room might have invited him. He dropped wearily into a chair near the door by which he had entered, and sat with his face half-hidden in the shadow of the pile of books.

"I am sorry you are going away," Marcia said, after a pause; "but—it is only for a short time, I hope; and yet you would scarcely disarrange your books unless you were leaving us for good."

"You are right, Miss Denison. I am going for good—or ill, perhaps. What a meaningless phrase that is, by the bye,—going away for good! Does any body ever go any where for good? I sometimes fancy that every step a man takes in life only carries him farther away from the chance of happiness; and that the Moslem alone is wise, who sits placidly upon his carpet and waits for his destiny."

"You are talking like papa," answered Marcia very gravely. "I should be very sorry if you were to learn to think like him."

"There are times when a thick darkness closes round a man's pathway, Miss Denison, and shuts out all the stars that have lighted his life. I am groping bewildered in such a darkness. I try still to hold by some guiding principle; but I am horribly shaken—I am horribly tempted. I have been reading the Book of Job lately. How easily I can believe in him; how well I can understand him! I fancy him sometimes in the dead of the night, as I sit alone in the chief room of some wayside inn, with a pistol-case within a few yards of me: so much alone that, if I were to be found dead the next morning, I should be found by strangers, who would only wonder at me as some melancholy lunatic who had strayed away from his keepers: so much alone that, if the news of my death were cried aloud all over the universe, there would not be a creature any the more sorrowful for the hearing of it."

"Mr. Pauncefort!"

There was a world of reproach in the tone.

"Oh, Miss Denison, I beg your pardon; but that is understood, of course," cried George Pauncefort, bitterly. "You would be sorry that one more self-murderer had gone red-handed to his doom. It is your *métier* to be sorry for sinners and poor people: but that is only Christianlike compassion, and not real human sorrow. There is scarcely a ruffian who ever went out of the debtor's-door who has not been regretted more truly by some one or other than ever I shall be regretted. Knowing this, can you wonder that I have learnt to recognise the sublimity of Job's patience? It is so easy to curse God, and die!"

"Mr. Pauncefort, you are breaking my heart!"

The words sounded almost like a cry. The tenant's moody face flushed and changed for a moment as he turned towards Marcia. He had been looking at the ground before, as with a kind of dogged determination not to look at her. The change was only momentary, and he bent his eyes down again with the same gloomy expression.

"I am a brute," he said, "to pain you with my troubles; but I have seen you listen so patiently to whining stories of unpaid rent and rheumatism. No unhappy wretch who ever lived in hourly fear of the bailiff's coming was ever more homeless than I am: and the pain that keeps me awake at night is a sharper torture than rheumatism."

"I am very sorry for you," said Marcia softly. There was a tenderness in the tone not to be mistaken for any conventional expression of compassion. George Pauncefort's heart thrilled at the sound of that tender music; but he kept his face still in shadow; and Marcia, looking towards

MISS DENISON'S HUMILIATION. 81

that part of the room where he sat, saw only a motionless figure, dark and gloomy as was the brooding sky without and the dusky chamber within.

"You are kind to be sorry for me," answered Mr. Pauncefort. "You said just now that you were glad—glad that I had returned; *I*—" He struck himself on the breast with a passionate gesture as he uttered the emphatic syllable. "To think that there should be any one upon earth glad for the coming of a desolate wretch like me, and to think *that* one should be you! Oh, if you could know how, for the moment, those simple words lifted me into a new life, and transformed me into a new creature! Miss Denison, it is not well for you and I to meet to-day. I lose all command of myself. There are moments in the life of the sanest man that ever lived in which he is as mad as the most dangerous lunatic in Bedlam. I am mad to-day. Let me wish you good-bye. Let me leave you with the knowledge that you have been sorry for a sorrow whose anguish you will never know. My books will be better company than myself. Let me leave you with them till your carriage comes."

He had risen, and had been walking up and down the room; but as he said this he advanced towards Marcia, holding out his hand. She gave him hers, and suffered it to lie passive in his grasp while she spoke to him.

"Mr. Pauncefort, why are you going to leave us?"

"Why!" he cried passionately. "Because I love you, Marcia Denison, more dearly than woman was ever loved before."

He let her hand fall from his, and fell on his knees before an empty chair. His head dropped on his arms, and with his face hidden thus, he knelt motionless, while Marcia stood a few paces from him staring aghast at that quiet figure so terribly expressive of despair. Even as she looked at him thus, full of that tender pity which was the most sublime element of her love, her womanly sense of trifles made her aware that the shabby coat which Dorothy had talked about was shabbier than of old; and she accepted it as the evidence of poverty which grew sharper day by day.

He loved her! His passionate confession brought her profound joy, but it gave her no surprise—she had so long been sure of his love; and looking back to the earliest period of their acquaintance, she knew that she had been loved from the very first.

But George Pauncefort's profound emotion alike mystified and alarmed her. The revelation of his love had been wrung from him like a cry of pain. Marcia, proud herself, could understand the pride of a penniless man who shrank from the avowal of a love whose disinterested purity might possibly be questioned; but she could not understand a pride so desperate as to deepen into such despair as that which George Pauncefort's manner had expressed to-day. She watched him wonderingly. Was he praying, or had he shrouded his face in order to conceal the tears a man sheds with such bitter shame? While Marcia was wondering about him, he rose, and walked towards the window. One glance at his face told her that there were no traces of tears upon it; but its gloomy blackness was more terrible than the expression of a man who has been weeping.

"I told you I was mad to-day, Miss Denison," he said; "you had better let me leave you to the companionship of my books." Though he said this, he made no attempt to leave the room; but stood with his face to the window, watching the leaves bending under the beating storm.

There was a pause of some minutes, in which every sound of the crackling fire, the dreary dripping rain, the rustling of the wet branches, was distinctly audible; and then Marcia went to the spot where her father's tenant was standing, and laid her hand lightly on his shoulder:

"You say that you are mad to-day," she said half playfully, but with so much earnestness under the lightness of her manner; "that is a bad compliment to me after what you said just now. Was there any truth in what you said, or is it only a part of your madness?"

"It is too fatally true, and it is the greater part of my madness."

He kept his face averted from her, and looked obstinately out at the rain as it came splashing heavily down on the low landscape, and shut out the dark distance, above which the thunder-clouds hung black and dense. Marcia paused a little before she addressed him again. Had he been any thing but what he was, had he been a prosperous man, her equal in years and in fortune, she would have perished rather than have invited him, by so much as one word or look, to speak to her when he was pleased to be silent, or remain with her when he wished to go. But then he was so much older than herself: he was so poor, so desolate. In his nine-and-thirty years, in his ruined fortunes, he might recognise two barriers which shut him from her—insuperable barriers which he could only cross by aid of her friendly hand held out towards him.

There is a pretty story of a rosebud given to her partner at a ball by the young Queen of England, in all the freshness of her girlish beauty—a partner who was afterwards the noblest model of what a gentleman and a husband should be. The story may be only a graceful invention, like that pretty speech about France and Frenchmen which a judicious reporter put into the mouth of Louis the Eighteenth; but the moral of the story is, that royalty must stoop a little when it sees itself worshipped by a heart that is too noble not to be proud. A woman with a large fortune has a kind of royalty of her own, and may stoop a little now and then without loss of dignity. Marcia Denison felt this. Perhaps it is in the nature of women to patronise; for her heart throbbed with a delicious sense of joy as she thought how much her wealth would do for the man she loved, if only she could summon courage to stoop low enough to lay her tribute at his feet.

If only she could summon courage!—there was the difficulty. Had she been a queen, the business would have been easy enough. But the quasi-royalty of an heiress is scarcely strong enough to bear such womanly humiliation without loss of dignity.

"I wonder at *his* pride, and yet I am so proud myself," she thought, with a half-smile upon her lips. And then, after a pause, she asked, as shyly as a child who blushes beneath the scrutinising glances of some stern godmother: "Are you going to leave England again, Mr. Pauncefort?"

"Yes, Miss Denison; I am going on one of my old exploring expeditions on the shores of the Niger. I am going in the footsteps of Barth and Livingstone. I scarcely wonder sometimes that Berkeley was sceptical as to the existence of any thing real or solid in all this universe. A man goes from one pole to another only to carry with him one idea, which is HIMSELF. Standing on the sands of the Dead Sea, groping blindly amidst a polar wilderness, in face of the awful grandeur of creation, the one mad passion of his life absorbs him still — the only reality amidst a world of shadows. All the verdure of the tropics, all the ice-bound solitudes of the arctic zone, serve only for a background to one figure — the inexorable Ego which reigns in the wanderer's breast. I talk nonsense, I daresay, Miss Denison; but sometimes when my life seems hardest to me, I begin to wonder whether, after all, I am only a shadow surrounded by shadows, and with nothing real around or about me, except the pain which I feel. I am in the mood to please your father just now. I would talk to him about Locke and Condillac to his heart's content."

"I am sorry for it," answered Marcia gently. "I have no taste for metaphysics, and to me it seems that the wisest of the metaphysicians, from St. Anselm to Bishop Berkeley, have been only splitters of shadowy straws, and triflers with the simplicity of truth. I thought the problem of life was solved eighteen hundred years ago, and I fancied that you were content to accept that solution."

"Yes, Miss Denison; but there are perilous moments even in the believer's life. Do you remember who it was that prayed, 'Help Thou mine unbelief'? Have you never felt one moment —I will not say of doubt, for that is too strong a word,—but one moment in which the faint shadow of a hideous hypothesis arose between you and the light, and you have thought, *if* it should not be true—*if* the story of Galilee should be only a beautiful idyl, a saga, a mythic image of grandeur, no more real than the legend of a William Tell? Satan seems to be an unfashionable personage in our modern theology; but depend upon it, he still holds his place among us, and whispers poisonous hints in our ears."

"I am sorry that your experience has revealed his existence to you."

"I have lived alone lately, and Satan has a partiality for the lonely. In the lives of the saints who were hermits you will find many records of his presence; but I don't think he often visited John Howard or Elizabeth Fry. I have been a solitary wanderer, and the fiend has made himself the companion of my walks. I come fresh from his company into yours; so you must not wonder if I seem a boor and a brute. You had better let me wish you good-bye, Miss Denison. Say farewell and 'God speed you!' to a wretch who goes out from the light of your presence into the dreariest darkness that ever lay between a ruined manhood and the grave."

He turned to leave the room, but before going held out his hand.

"You will shake hands with me," he said. "I know how churlish a return I seem to have made for your father's hospitable friendliness and your compassionate regard; but I have my secret. If you knew it, I do not think you would wonder that I am what I am."

He took Marcia's hand in his and pressed it gently. After that he would have released it; but the soft loving fingers clung to his, not to be repulsed, and a second detaining hand was laid gently on his wrist.

Held thus, and rooted to the spot by the sudden wonder that filled his mind, he gazed at the earnest face turned towards him,—the pale pensive face that to him seemed to be bright with a supernal glory.

"Why do you force me to speak to you?" said Marcia. "Why do you make me say that which should have come from your lips, and from yours alone? Do you think so meanly of me that you fear I should misunderstand you; or are you so proud that you cannot stoop to accept any advantage from a woman's hands? You tell me that you love me—ah, and I know you tell me only the truth—yet at the same moment you say you are going to leave me—for ever perhaps; to die some horrible death in a foreign country, nameless and uncared for! I have read so much about Africa since I have known you, and my heart freezes with horror when I think of you, wandering alone in that dreadful country. Oh, George Pauncefort! if your love is worthy of the name of love, it must be more precious to you than your pride; and yet you would sacrifice your love to your pride. I have fancied myself proud: but see how low I stoop for your sake— for your sake!"

"Stop, Marcia!" cried Sir Jasper's tenant, drawing his hand from her gentle grasp and at the same time recoiling from her,—" stop, for pity's sake!"

He fell on his knees at her feet, with his head

bent to the very dust and his clasped hands lifted above it.

"I will not stop! Your obstinate pride would have separated us for ever; and you would go out into the world doubting even in Heaven rather than you would bend the haughty spirit that rebels against the merest shadow of an obligation. If I had loved you, and been loved by you, years ago in my girlhood, I should have let you go in silence —to break my heart when you were gone. But we are no children, Mr. Pauncefort, to trifle with the chance of happiness that Heaven has given us. I am a woman, and my lonely, loveless life has taught me what a precious gift Heaven bestows when it gives a woman the affection of one honest heart. I will not lose your love; I will not sacrifice the chance of helping you to regain all that you have lost, for lack of courage to speak a few plain words, whatever sacrifice I make in speaking them. You love me,—if you had never said that, I could never have spoken,—but you *have* said that you love me, and the rest is easy. I know your secret; to me your life seems so transparent: your ruined hopes—your broken fortunes—your poverty, so proudly endured. I know all, George; and I ask you to let my money—my poor paltry money, gained in the honest pathways of commerce — restore your name, retrieve your broken life. Oh, George, tell me you are not too proud to accept the happiness which my fortune may bring back to you—the fortune that I never valued until I knew you were poor."

She covered her face with her outspread hands to hide the hot blushes that dyed it with so deep a crimson. With her face covered thus, she waited for him to answer her. For some moments he was silent; then, rising slowly from his knees, he said in a low broken voice, so low as to be almost a whisper:

"You are quite mistaken as to my story. There is no landed squire in this county richer in the world's wealth than I am. Oh, Miss Denison, how will you ever forgive me, when you know what I thought might be hidden from you for ever, but which must be told you now!"

Marcia dropped her hands from before her face,

and looked at her lover. He was standing a few paces from her, with his face turned towards the light. In all her life she had never seen such a mortal pallor as that which she saw now in the dark face she loved. But in the depth of her humiliation, this only struck her in a confused way. The justification of her conduct was suddenly snatched away from her; all the theory of her life was shattered. Her father's tenant was not poor! She had not stooped from the dignity of her womanhood to elevate a lowly suitor, whose proud humility was the only barrier that divided him from her. It was all so much wasted degradation. Impelled by an unconsidered impulse, she had flung her maidenly pride into the dust at this man's feet. She had asked him—yes, asked him to accept her hand and her fortune! Only a few minutes had elapsed since she had spoken, and yet she thought of her own words with shame and wonder. She had besought him to accept a hand which he did not care to demand for himself; a fortune which he did not want. Tears rose to her eyes—the passionate tears of wounded pride. She drew herself up with an involuntary movement of offended dignity, and went back to the hearth, where her bonnet and shawl had been hung to dry.

"I think the storm is nearly over now, Mr. Pauncefort," she said quietly. "Will you be good enough to see if the carriage has come?"

"Yes, Marcia; but not yet. You have spoken to me; and I must speak to you. Oh, my darling, my love!—let me call you thus once, and once only: when you pass the threshold of this house a few minutes hence, you will have bid good-bye to me for ever!—have you never thought of any other reason than poverty for my lonely life, my dull despair? Oh, Marcia, how little you have known me, after all!—you, who have dropped such balm into my wounds, who have given me such tender comfort for my sorrows,—how little you have known me, when you can think that poverty was the evil that made my life a burden to me! Poverty! pshaw; a rough honest friend, and not an enemy; a companion Diogenes, who strips the mask off earth's conventionalities, and points out the few true men among the knaves. To a weak sensuous nature poverty may be terrible; for it takes another name, and calls itself deprivation—unsatiated thirst for impossible pleasures, the torture of Tantalus. But for me poverty has no terrors. Ah, if you knew how often in my lonely walks I have listened to the blacksmith beating at his glowing furnace, and have envied him his labour, his light heart, and his empty pockets! Do you think so meanly of me as to suppose that, if poverty were my only trouble, I would sit in this room, when I might go out into the world and fight for one of the thousand prizes that Fortune holds for the head that thinks, and the hand that works? No, Miss Denison, I am a rich man; and the gulf which yawns between you and me is a wider gulf than any division created by difference of fortune."

Marcia looked at him with something like terror in her face. She had trusted him so entirely; she had heard him accused, and her faith had been unshaken. Serene in her instinctive confidence, she had smiled at Blanche Harding's ominous hints;

and now all at once her heart sank, for it seemed as if those dark insinuations were about to receive confirmation from his own lips. Yes, it must be so. The gulf between them was this man's dishonour — his dishonour! And amidst the tempestuous ocean of passion on which her soul had been tossed to and fro, her only anchor had been her faith in him.

She put up her hand with a piteously-imploring gesture, as if she would have arrested any confession that was about to escape his lips.

"Oh, do not tell me that you are any thing less than I have thought you!" she cried; "I have believed so entirely in your goodness, your truth, your honour. If I have been deceived until now, let the deception go on for ever. I cannot bear to think that it is any shame or disgrace which has banished you from the world."

"Marcia Denison," answered Sir Jasper's tenant, "there are people who have to bear the burden of dishonours in which they have had no part. There are social laws which revenge on the innocent the wicked deeds of the guilty. The name I have a right to bear was disgraced fifteen years ago; but by no act of mine. I went to sleep one night a proud ambitious man, with all the world before me, and with sustaining faith and energy that help a man to win the noblest prizes earth can give. I woke the next morning to find myself what you see me now—a thing without a hope, without a name,—too glad to hide my ruin from the world in which I had once held myself so proudly."

He covered his face with his hands. While his eyes were darkened thus, he felt Marcia's loving fingers trying to loosen those strong hands from the face they shrouded.

"The disgrace came by no act of yours," she murmured softly; "ah, I knew, I knew that *you* were true and noble! George, if you love me, dishonour may sully your name, but it shall never affect me. Women have borne dishonoured names before to-day. Give me yours, George: it shall be a more precious gift to me than the loftiest title that ever was worn upon this earth. George, why do you force me to say what you have a right to despise me for saying?"

"Despise you, Marcia! Oh, I am the guiltiest, basest wretch that ever lived. It is so hard, so hard for me to speak the truth! God, who only knows the weight and measure of the tortures He inflicts, knows how I love you, and how fiercely I have struggled against the growth of my love. The confession of my love is an insult to you, Marcia. My passion itself is a crime. My life for the last fifteen years has been a lie, and the name I have borne is a false one. My name is Godfrey Pierrepoint, and I am the dishonoured husband of a guilty wife!"

Never had Sir Jasper's tenant seen in any countenance such a depth of sorrowful reproach as that which looked at him now out of the tender gray eyes he loved so well.

"And you have let me love you," said Marcia; "and you have let me speak to you of my love! Oh, what shame, what shame, what shame!"

She hurried towards the door with her arms stretched before her like a half-demented creature who flies from some unspeakable horror; but on the very threshold, before George Pauncefort could save her, Sir Jasper's daughter fell prone upon the very spot whereon the country people were wont to point triumphantly to the blood-bespattered traces of the murdered cavalier.

CHAPTER V.

FAREWELL.

When Marcia lifted her heavy eyelids and awoke from that sudden swoon, she found herself seated in the worm-eaten oak chair, with the open doorway before her, and the air blowing in upon her with a damp freshness that was better than all the eau-de-cologne that ever an indefatigable abigail bespattered over a fainting mistress. At first the fresh cool air brought Miss Denison nothing but a delicious sense of relief from something very like suffocation. Then came a consciousness of external things; she heard the rustling of the leaves and the pawing and champing of a horse at the garden-gate, and knew that the carriage had arrived. Last of all there returned to her, with unspeakable bitterness, the knowledge of why she had fainted, and what had happened before her fainting-fit.

"Oh, my God!" she thought in her despair; "there has been so little joy in my life, but I have never suffered like this until to-day."

For the moment she did not attempt to move, but sat with her eyelids drooping and her eyes fixed upon the floor with an almost stupid look. She felt a strange disinclination to stir, to take any step in the progress of her broken life. If it could have ended there, at that moment!

"I am so little use in the world; nobody loves me, nobody has any need of me," she thought piteously; "my life is only a penance. What sin did I commit when I was a child, that I should suffer so much in my womanhood? And it is wicked even to wish to die."

She was aroused from her sense of utter prostration by the voice of the man she loved. It struck upon her as sharply as the lash of a whip; and she looked up at George Pauncefort, stung into sudden life.

"I want you to say that you forgive me," he

began, in a low sad voice, "and then I shall be brave enough to bid you farewell for ever."

She did not answer him immediately; but after a pause she said, "Do you know how deeply you have humiliated me?"

"I have not humiliated you. There can be no humiliation for such a nature as yours. You have spoken the noblest words that ever a woman uttered. Unhappily, you have spoken them to a man who has no right to hear them. The crime and the shame were his. I know now that it was the basest cowardice which prompted me to keep my secret. But oh, Marcia, how could I think that you would stoop to love me! How could I believe that your tender compassion for a ruined life could ever grow into any thing grander and holier than compassion! And even now, though your own lips have said so much, can I be quite sure that the impulse which stirred them was not the generous pity of a noble heart—the self-abnegation of a woman who offers her richest treasure to a beggar? That you can love me—*me!* O God, it cannot be real! It is too like my dreams."

Marcia uttered no word in response to that passionate outburst; but after a pause, she said quietly:

"Will you take me to the carriage, Mr. Pauncefort?—I must still call you by that name. Papa will be uneasy about me, perhaps, and I am quite ready to go back."

She rose, but Sir Jasper's tenant laid his hand upon her arm.

"For pity's sake, forgive me," he said. "I shall leave this place at daybreak to-morrow, to go to the other end of the world, perhaps. I *cannot* go without your forgiveness; I cannot—I cannot. Think me a good Christian if I do not kill myself to-night. I have suffered too much lately. Yes, Marcia, some burdens are too heavy. Say that you forgive me, and let me go back to the solitudes out yonder, where no one who is interested in my death can track me, and where, if I go mad, there will be no one to put me into a madhouse. Marcia, forgive me!"

He fell on his knees. His passionate violence, the despair that was so nearly akin to madness, awoke all that was most womanly in Mareia Denison's nature. She bent over the dark face that was lifted towards her, distorted and convulsed by the agony of a passion that had burst all the bonds of reason. She laid her hand softly on the burning forehead, and parted the tumbled hair as gently as ever motherly hands tended a sick child.

"Forgive you!" she murmured; "I have nothing to forgive. It was a false pride that made me so angry. There can be no question of humiliation between you and me. We are both too unhappy. Give me your hand, and let us say good-bye."

"Good-bye, Mareia. My bright ideal of womanhood, good-bye."

He rose and offered her his hand. The storm had gone by without; the storm was lulled within; George Pauncefort was himself again, grave and sombre, with only a quiet look of sorrow in his face.

"You will bear your burden bravely?" said Mareia, questioningly. "Yes, I know you will. You are too good a Christian to feel often as you have felt to-day. Oh, believe me, there is no burden too heavy; divine endurance has measured the weight of all; and we have only to be patient. Promise me you will try to support your sorrows like a Christian."

"For your sake, Marcia! Ask me to do anything for your sake, and the doing of it shall be the business of my life. There is no difference between love and fanaticism."

"You will try to be a Christian for my sake?"

"Yes, Marcia, as I hope to be saved—for your sake. There is no such thing as myself in the world henceforward; there is nothing but you, and my love for you. But I am going to be a Christian to please you; and my first sacrifice shall be to bid you good-bye."

"Good-bye. I shall pray for you every night and morning, as I should pray for my brother, if I had one."

"Only one word more, Marcia. You have asked me nothing of my past life. And if you had questioned me, I scarcely think that I could have brought myself to speak of that shameful story in your presence. Yet I should like you to know it. I have made it the business of my existence to escape from what people call sympathy; but I should like to have your pity. I will write the story, Marcia. Will you read it?"

"Yes. Once more, good-bye."

They were on the threshold as Marcia spoke; and as she stepped from that narrow threshold a sudden gleam of yellow sunlight shot forth upon the edge of a cloud, and shone reflected on her face as she turned towards her father's tenant.

George Pauncefort uttered a cry of triumph.

"See, Marcia," he exclaimed; "the sun shines upon us! I was never superstitious until to-day; but to-day I will believe any thing that hints at a hope. I accept the omen, Marcia. This parting is not for ever."

She did not answer him. Her calm sorrow had no affinity with his feverish exaltation of spirit, and was not subject to any abrupt transition from despair to hope. To her it seemed as if the dull horizon of her life had only opened for a moment, to reveal a glimpse of an impossible heaven, and to close again for ever. Already she was resigned to the thought that George Pauncefort could never be any more to her than he had been during the last few months. And it seemed as if he had been so much to her; for he had been, and he must for ever be, the one creature to whom she had been precious; the only being who had ever been profoundly affected with either joy or sorrow for her sake; the solitary friend; the only lover: an image never to be disturbed from his place in her heart.

George Pauncefort handed his guest into her carriage. The sunlight had burst forth in fuller glory, beautiful on the deep-green of the wet leaves and the tender emerald of the fern; supernally beautiful on the latticed casements of the Hermitage, and on the shining surface of the pool.

In this sunlight, and in the wondrous tranquillity of earth and sky that succeeds a summer tempest, Sir Jasper's tenant and Sir Jasper's daughter parted.

It was not until the next evening that Marcia received a packet, which had been left in Mrs.

Tursgood's charge when George Pauncefort and his servant quitted the Hermitage. It was a large parcel, containing some rare old books that Miss Denison had once expressed a wish to possess, and its arrival excited no particular attention; but hidden amongst the quaintly-bound volumes there was a packet in a large envelope, addressed to Marcia, and signed with George Pauncefort or Godfrey Pierrepoint's initials. Miss Denison opened the parcel late at night, in her own room, and the first chill glimmer of day found her still reading Mr. Pauncefort's letter.

CHAPTER VI.

THE STORY OF A YOUNG MAN'S FOLLY.

"SHALL I tell you what I felt, Marcia, when first you beckoned me into your father's room, and I sat in the dusk looking at you, with the warm glow of the fire about your figure, and the fitful light shining every now and then upon your face? There is no such thing as love at first sight; for I did not love you then. The feelings that stirred my heart as it was stirred that night belonged only to the strange atmosphere I had entered. You can never understand *how* strange that room and its belongings were to me. No terror of the desert, no peril from savage beasts or treacherous men would have moved me half so keenly as I was moved by this one glimpse of an English home. And for yourself, Marcia, what were you to me then—you who have since become the universe?

How I wonder as I remember that night, when I only thought of you with a calm, artistic pleasure, as a connoisseur thinks of a beautiful picture!

"Let no man ever neglect the warning of his instinct. From the first my instinct told me that the delicious happiness I found in your presence, in your father's society,—ah, how persistently I cheated myself as to the *real* source of my pleasure!—from the very first I was conscious of peril: but the temptation was too great. I could not resign the happiness. It was so easy to cheat myself. When your image shone brightest before my eyes, I thought, 'If I had been a happier man, I might have had such a creature for my daughter: there are men who have had such women for their wives.' Again and again I reminded myself that I was almost old enough to be your father; again and again I deluded myself by the old shallow lies with which a weak man palters with his conscience. A weak man; and I had thought myself so strong until I knew you!

"It was only when I had been an inmate of

your father's house, and found how horrible a pang it was to me to go back to the darkness of my old life—it was only then that I knew I loved you. It was only when I sat alone in my desolate room, recalling every look of your face, every tone of your voice, maddened with the memory of them, and the knowledge that I had no right to see your face or hear your voice again—it was then only that I knew the intensity of my love, and how little hope there was that my wretched heart would ever know its old dull quiet again. God knows how I struggled against my temptation: you know how I succumbed to it. I should have gone back to the desert—back to the lonely marches and the weary haltings under a torrid sky; but the tempter was too strong for me. The cup which he offered to my lips was so sweet. From first to last I knew that it was poison—from first to last I drank the insidious draught, knowing that there was death at the bottom of it.

"Had I no thought for you in all this? Yes, I thought of you with cruel anguish as I fancied how compassionately you would smile at my folly if the knowledge of it could reach you. I watched you too closely not to fancy myself master of every thought and feeling of yours. Your reverential kindness, your courteous attention, the sympathy which you evinced for my favourite studies, the pleasure you appeared to take in my conversation,—to me these seemed only the natural graces of a perfect creature, whose divine compassion extended itself even to a gloomy middle-aged man whose broken life rendered him an object of pity.

"In all the regions of the impossible could there be any thing so wild as the thought that you could love me—*me?* Can I imagine or understand the possibility even now? No, my soul and life! only in my dreams—only in my dreams can I believe in so deep a joy. But I have no right to speak to you of this. I have no right to approach you in any character but that of an unhappy wretch who has need of your pity.

"If I could have known you in my early manhood—when life was bright before me—when in all the world there was no height so lofty that it seemed impossible to my ambitious fancies! I think ambition is only another name for youth, and that a man who has never been ambitious has never been young. I was the only son of a younger son. My father and mother were both what the world calls 'highly connected,' but they were both poor. You will think perhaps that I am going to burst forth into some grand tirade upon the horrors of poverty; but you need have no such apprehension. The poverty of my boyhood had no horrors, for it was endured by souls too lofty to droop under the influence of shabby clothes or indifferent dinners. I have seen my mother dine in a cotton gown, but I have never seen her quail before the presence of a creditor. I have seen my father in a threadbare dresscoat hob-nobbing with a marquis, and looking as much a marquis as his companion. There is something noble in the old races, after all. Set a Pierrepoint to sweep a crossing, and he will sweep it like a Pierrepoint; so that passers-by shall glance back at him and mutter, 'A nobleman in disguise.' Do not laugh at me, Marcia, because I have clung to those foolish fancies of my youth amidst the ruin of my manhood. My mother's race was noble, but her love for my father changed into reverence when she thought of his name; and it was on her knee that I learned how grand a thing it was to be a Pierrepoint.

"My father was a philosopher, a linguist, a collector of rare old editions and curious pamphlets; every thing that a man can be who believes that all the happiness of life is comprised in the verb 'to know.' In all my memory of him, I can never recall his being interested in any event of our everyday life, or the lives of our neighbours. We lived in an old tumble-down house, which had once been a vicarage. The old churchyard sloped westward below our drawing-room windows, and my first memory is of the crimson sunlight behind dark masses of wreathing ivy, which I knew afterwards were hidden graves; but the church had not been standing for the last hundred years. Our garden adjoined this grassy enclosure, and I played sometimes among the rose- and currant-bushes, sometimes among the ivy-hidden tombs that had once been stately monuments. The house belonged to my uncle Weldon, the head of our family, and we lived in it rent-free. All around us, wherever our eyes could reach, the land we saw was Weldon Pierrepoint's, and had been in the possession of Pierrepoints from the days of Stephen. The village nearest to us was called Pierrepoint, and I was seven years old before I passed the boundary of my uncle's estate.

"If we had lived any where else, we might, perhaps, have been made to feel that there is some sting in poverty. At Pierrepoint, the man who hesitated to doff his hat as my father passed him would have been scouted as a kind of infidel. Our own name, and my uncle's wealth, covered us with a kind of halo; and when my mother went through the village-street in her straw bonnet and cotton dress, her promenade was like a royal progress. Thus, from my very childhood, I learned to believe that it was a grand thing to be what I was; and when I was old enough to know what poverty meant, I laughed to scorn the suggestion that it could be any hindrance to my success in life.

"My first misfortune was perhaps the fact that I lived too long at Pierrepoint—too exclusively among people who respected me for the associations of my name—too far away from the open field of life, in which Jones the baker's son has as good a chance of victory and loot as the direct descendant of the Plantagenets. My mother and father were equally ignorant of the world beyond Pierrepoint Castle and Pierrepoint Grange. My parents were too poor to give me a university career; and as my father's learning would have been enough to divide among all the professors of a college, it was naturally supposed that I could need no better teacher; so I was educated at home. I know now that I could not have had a worse tutor, and that the key to my broken life is to be found in the narrow school of my boyhood. Under my father's tuition, I became a sage in book-lore, and remained a baby in all worldly knowledge. Heaven only knows what dreams have visited me in that old walled garden, where the grass grew deeper and softer than any verdure I have ever trodden on since. What visions of worldly greatness to be won far away in the unknown region, where so many crowns hung within the reach of daring hands. What vivid pictures of a successful career—of prizes to be won while all the bloom of youth was yet upon the winner—of a sharp brief struggle with fortune, and a garland of fame to be brought home to that very garden and laid at my mother's feet. Every boy brought up very quietly with gentle people, amidst a pastoral landscape, is apt to fancy himself an embryo Wellington or Nelson. My childish yearnings were for a soldier's life, and I pictured myself coming back, after the conquest of India, to Pierrepoint Grange, to marry the curate's blue-eyed daughter, who was so desperate a coquette in haymaking-time. God help me now, in my desolation and hopelessness! I can bring back the very picture I made of myself, riding up to the low white gate on a cavalry charger and dressed in a general's uniform!

"All these dreams melted away when I grew

a little older, and my father had imbued me with something of his own love of learning. There were many consultations with my rich uncle as to my future career, and I found that the question was regarded less with a view to my interests than with reference to what a Pierrepoint might or might not do without damage to the other Pierrepoints. After a great deal of deliberation it was settled that a Pierrepoint need undergo no degradation in being created Lord Chancellor, and it was thereupon decided that I should be called to the bar. Weldon Pierrepoint, my uncle, had sons of his own, and his property seemed as far away from me as if I had been a stranger to his blood; but I was his nephew, and his only nephew, so he volunteered to allow me a small income while I studied, and endeavoured to work my way in the legal profession. His offer was accepted; and I went up to London by a mail-coach with letters of introduction to some of the highest people in the metropolis in my desk, and with five-and-twenty pounds, the first quarterly payment of my income, in my pocket.

" You would smile, Marcia, if you could know how intoxicating to me was the consciousness that I was stepping out into the battle-field, how implicit my faith in my power to win fame and fortune. The introductions I carried with me would have obtained me a footing in half the best drawing-rooms of the West-end; but the only one of my credentials of which I made any use was a letter addressed to an octogenarian legal celebrity, who lived by himself in the Temple, and who had the finest law-library and the best collection of Hobbimas in England. This gentleman received me with civility; told me that I looked like a Pierrepoint; warned me against the dissipations of London, which were all very well for common people, but not fit for Pierrepoints; and put me in the way of beginning my new life. Under his advice I selected a couple of garrets, which were dignified by the name of chambers, and I looked on with profound satisfaction while the name of Pierrepoint was inscribed in white paint on a black door, immediately below the leaking ceiling that had been discoloured by the rain-drip of about half a century. Ah, what a boy I was! I plunged into the severest course of legal study that I could devise for myself; and the sparrows twittered every day in the morning sunshine before I closed my books and went to bed. I hired a lad, who cleaned my boots and brushed my clothes, and who was to open my door in case, by some extraordinary combination of circumstances, any one should ever come to knock at it; and I employed a laundress, who cleaned my rooms and bought my provisions. I have dined for a fortnight at a stretch on no better dinner than a mutton-chop, and no stronger beverage than tea; and I have lived for a month sometimes without interchanging a word with any creature except the laundress or the boy.

"Ah, what a foolish dreamer I was, Marcia! I fancied that my life was in my own hands, and that in my own untiring energy, my own love of learned labours, there lay the powers that could mould me into a Bacon, without a Bacon's vices; a second Brougham, with more than a Brougham's greatness. In my garret, with sickly candles fading in a sickly dawn, I fancied myself at the summit of Fame's mighty mountain, with all the world below me. The vision of the future was infinitely more real to me than any penalties of the present. I began to suffer from chronic headache; but I wrapped a wet towel round my forehead, and laughed my malady to scorn. If Homer had knocked-under to a headache, the *Iliad* might never have been finished. If Bacon had not been superior to physical pains, the world might have lost the *Novum Organon*. What mighty shadows visited me in my attic chambers! I have never seen them since. The Rosicrucians believe that the grandest mysteries of their faith reveal themselves only to the pure gaze of the celibate. An earthly face was soon to come between me and the faces of my dreams.

"I had lived a year in London—a long, lonely year, broken by no home-visit; for though I pined for the sight of my mother's face, I could not go back to Pierrepoint until I had advanced by some small step upon the great high-road I was so pleased to tread,—I had been in London a year, and my spirit was as fresh as when I left home; but the dull commonplace machine—the body—which will do no more work for a Bacon than for a baker, broke down. I had an attack of low fever, which was not entirely free from danger; and the doctor who attended me told me that if I wished to live and to go on working, I must give myself a summer holiday in the country, and close my books for some weeks. My first impulse was to go to Pierrepoint; but when I looked at myself in the glass, and saw the ghastly-looking face reflected there, I felt that it would be a cruelty to alarm my mother by presenting myself before her until I had recovered a little of the strength I had wasted so recklessly in my daily and nightly labours. My going back to Pierrepoint might have imperilled my future career; for one of the tenderest mothers that ever lived would perhaps have taken fright at my altered looks, and dissuaded me from pursuing my legal studies.

"I loved my mother very dearly; but I could not endure the idea of sacrificing my ambition even for her sake. So I did not go to Pierrepoint; and the bright dream of my future was wrested from me by a wicked woman instead of being voluntarily surrendered to a good one.

"Instead of going to my dear old home in the remotest depths of Yorkshire, I went to a little village on the very edge of London. I have done battle all my life against the insidious doctrine of fatalism; but I find myself wondering sometimes why it was I chose that one village from amongst so many places of the same character, and how it was that such a multiplicity of small circumstances conspired to bring about my going there. The place was not a popular resort. It lay quite away from the beaten track; and I had never seen the name of it until I dropped down upon the rustic green one summer's day, and read the inscription on a sign-post. I had wandered listlessly from the Temple to the City early that morning, and had taken a place in the first coach that left the neighbourhood of the Bank, too indifferent to inquire where it would take me. How well I remember the hot summer's day; the light upon the village green, where there were ducks splashing in a pond, and pigeons strutting before a low-roofed inn; the sheltered beauty of a glade that led away to the church; the richly wooded landscape sloping westward in the distance; and above all, the delicious sense of repose that hung about the place like a palpable atmosphere, and soothed my shattered nerves into drowsy quiet! The place was so near London, in fact, that I wondered not to hear the roaring thunder of wheels booming across that woodland slope; yet in all semblance so remote from bustle and clamour, that I might have fancied myself in the most pastoral district of my native county. I decided at once that this was the spot in which I might recruit my strength, without going far away from the scene of my labour; and the only question was whether I could get a lodging. I inquired at the little inn, before which the pigeons were strutting, and was told that I could be accommodated there with rooms that, despite their rustic simplicity, were infinitely more luxurious than my chambers in the Temple. The village was only a cluster of four or five handsome old houses, with a halting-place for man and beast on the green, a pond for the ducks, a signpost for the enlightenment of strayed wanderers, and a tiny church half hidden by the yew-trees that overshadowed it. There was a blacksmith's forge next door to the little inn, and there were two or three old-fashioned cottages with little gardens before them, in which mignonette and geraniums grew luxuriantly. In all the place there was only one lodging to be had, and that was the one I took. If that had been occupied, I must have gone to seek a resting-place elsewhere; and then the whole of my life since that hour would have been different from what it has been. I try not to remember upon what a gossamer-thread the balance of my fate swung to and fro that day when I dawdled on the village green and lounged in the village public-house.

"I did not go back to London. I had no friends of whom to take leave, no social engagements from which to excuse myself, no debts to pay; all the money I possessed in the world was in my pocket. I wrote a line to my laundress, telling her where to send my portmanteau, and despatched it by the return coach; and having done this, all my arrangements were made, and I was free to saunter out on the green, with my hands in my pockets, and breathe some of the fresh air that was to refit me for my work in London.

"I went out, weak still, but not listless; for it would have been strange indeed if the aspect of a summer landscape had not been very pleasant to me after the chimney-pots I had looked at so long. The sun was dropping down behind the lower edge of the western slope, and a faint crimson glory touched the water at my feet, and flickered among the leaves of the great dark beeches in the glade. For the moment I forgot that I was an embryo Lord Chancellor. Bacon and Montesquieu might never have existed, for any place they had in my mind. The *De Augmentis*, the *Readings on the Statutes of Uses*, the *Esprit des Lois*, might never have been written, for any influence they had upon my thoughts. I was a boyish dreamer, intoxicated with the beauty of the scene around me, and ready to burst forth into rapturous quotations from Keats or Shelley, as every new glimpse of the lovely landscape burst upon me. For twelve months I had been a recluse in a London garret; for twelve months I had seen nothing brighter than the chrysanthemums in the Temple gardens.

"I walked slowly along with my hands in my pockets, whispering quotations from the *Revolt of Islam*, between the two grand lines of beech and elm, growing so close together that the path between them was a densely-shadowed green passage rather than a common avenue; a long arcade, odorous with a faint aromatic perfume, and narrowing in the distance to one little spot where the yellow light shone like a star. I emerged from the avenue into this warm evening sunshine, and found myself close to the low white gate of the churchyard.

"The sound of the organ came floating out through the open windows of the little church, and I stopped at the gate to listen. Of all sounds upon earth, that of an organ is to my ear the holiest music. If I were an infidel all the rest of my life, I should be a true believer while I listened to the music of a church-organ. A Protestant among Roman Catholics—kneeling amidst the shadowy splendour of Cologne, or Antwerp, or Rouen, I have been as true a Romanist as the most bigoted of my companions while the glorious harmonies of Mozart rapt my soul in a trance of delight. I stood with my arms folded on the gate, and listened to the organ of Weldridge church as I have listened since to grander music in so many splendid temples. The organ was not a good one; but it was well played. The musician possessed taste and feeling; the music was from Beethoven's *Mount of Olives*. I listened until the last sound of the organ died away, and I was still lingering with the dreamy spell of the music full upon me, when it was exorcised by quite a different sound—the silvery laughter of a woman ringing out upon the air.

"And then I heard a clear voice cry, 'Thank you, Mr. Scott; but it really is the vilest old organ. Why doesn't the rector get up a subscription, and preach sermons, and plan a concert or fancy-fair, or something of that kind, and get a new instrument? It really is horrible. However, it was very kind of you to let me play; and I had such an absurd mania for trying that organ. But I always want to try every piano I see; and I do think if I were visiting at Buckingham Palace, and there were a piano in the room, I should whisk up to it, and run a double chromatic scale from the bottom to the top. Imagine the Queen's feelings! A chromatic scale is more hideous than any thing in the world, except the howling of melancholy cats.'

"There was a low masculine growl after this; and then the clear voice broke out again: 'Do you really think so? Well, I'm sure it's very kind of you to say so. I was educated at a convent, you know—not that I'm a Catholic—oh, dear, no! Papa always sent particular orders about my opinions not being biassed every time he paid the half-yearly bills; and I used to play the organ in our convent-chapel; but I never played to a real congregation in a real church. It would be such—I suppose I musn't say fun; but it really would be nice. However, papa will be waiting for dinner if I don't take care, and then I shall be scolded. Good afternoon.'

"Then came a light pattering of feet, the flutter of a muslin dress, the resonant bang of a heavy door; and the prettiest woman I had ever seen in my life came tripping along the churchyard path towards the very gate on which I was leaning.

"The prettiest woman I had ever seen in my life. Yes; it was in the form of Beauty's brightest ideal that Caroline Catheron appeared to my foolish eyes. I had seen so few women, I had so vague an idea of what lovely and lovable womanhood should be. This bright creature, who chatted and laughed with the gray-headed old organist, and shook out her airy muslin scarf as she tripped towards me,—this beaming young beauty, whose dark eyes flashed with a happy consciousness of their own brilliancy,—this queen of roses and lilies,—this splendid belle, whose image might have shone upon a dreaming sultan amidst a throng of shadowy houris,—this holiday idol, to be set up for the worship of fools and profligates—seemed to me the incarnation of feminine loveliness. My heart did not thrill then as it has thrilled since at the lowest murmur of one loved voice; my soul's purest depths lay far below this woman's power to stir them; but my eyes were dazzled by this living, breathing splendour of form and colour, and my rapt gaze followed Caroline Catheron as if the little parasol she held so lightly in her hand had been the wand of an enchantress. I opened the gate for her, and stood aside to let her pass. She thanked me with the prettiest inclination of her head, and tripped away under the trees with the old organist by her side. I made a paltry pretence of going into the churchyard and looking at the tombstones; and after keeping up this pretence for about five minutes, I followed the organist and his companion.

"They were talking. The girl's voice rang clearly out in the stillness—silvery as the singing of the birds in the woodland round about us. Her talk was commonplace and frivolous enough; but for the last twelve months I had rarely heard any sweeter feminine tones than the hoarse snuffle of my laundress: and I followed and listened, enthralled by this clear music of a pretty woman's voice, which was so very new to me. She was talking about her papa,—what he liked and what he did not like; how he was an epicure, and it was so difficult to get any thing tolerable for dinner in Weldridge; how he could scarcely exist without his newspapers, and how the newspapers often arrived so very late at Weldridge; how he was beginning to grow tired of the place already, in spite of its rustic beauty, and was thinking of leaving it very soon. My heart sank as I heard this. All the glory of my holiday would vanish with this beautiful creature, whom I had only seen within the last quarter of an hour. From the organist's replies to the young lady's speeches I understood that her father's name was Catheron. Catheron! It sounded like a good name, I thought, and it was something at least to know her name; but oh, how I wondered by what blessed combination of small chances I should ever come to know this wondrous being, who was as gracious to the old organist in his shabby week-day clothes as if he had been a duke! I wondered which of the stately mansions at Weldridge sheltered this divinity. I wondered in what umbrageous gardens she dawdled away her days, fairer than the fairest flower that ever blossomed upon this earth. There were several grand old houses at Weldridge—secluded habitations embowered in foliage, and only revealing themselves by a clock-tower, a quaint old stone cupola, or a stack of gothic chimneys peeping through a break in the wood.

"My divinity and her companion went by the stately gates, and under the shadow of the lofty walls; they went to the very end of the leafy passage, and then emerged and walked briskly across the green, where an unkempt pony and a drowsy-looking donkey were cropping the short grass in listless contentment. They crossed the green; the young lady parted from her companion before one of the row of cottages near the inn at which I was to spend my holiday. She dropped the organist a pretty little curtsey, opened the wooden gate, and went into the rustic garden. I watched her till the cottage-door had opened and ingulfed her. She was my neighbour. My heart gave a great leap at the very thought; and I went back to my lodging filled with a happiness that was new to me—a strange, intoxicating kind of happiness; like the drunkenness of a boy who has tasted champagne for the first time.

"Why do I tell you these things, Marcia? Is this the vivisection of my own heart at which I am assisting so coolly? No! I, who exist to-day, have no share in the nature of this young law-student who fell in love with Caroline Catheron seventeen years ago. I am only telling you of the foolish infatuation of a foolish boy, who mistook the capricious impulses of his fancy for the true instincts of his heart.

"I went back to my lodging, and made a ridiculous pretence of eating the meal — half-dinner, half-supper—that had been prepared for me. I was still weak from the effects of my fever; and after this attempt I sat in an easy-chair by the open window, looking out at the dusky landscape, above which the stars were shining faintly. A gray mist had crept over the neighbouring woodland and the distant hills, and lights were gleaming here and there in the windows of one of the Weldridge mansions. At another time I should have been eager for a candle and a book, and impatient of this useless twilight; but upon this particular night I think I forgot that I had ever been a student. All the mighty shadows of my life had vanished, and across the dim gray mist I saw a woman's face looking at me with a bright coquettish smile. I abandoned myself to a delicious reverie, in which I fancied my beautiful neighbour tending an invalid father—hovering about an idolised mother; a creature of life and light in that simple household; a being from whose presence joy emanated as naturally as the perfume emanates from the flower. If the impossible Asmodeus had taken me out amongst the chimneys of the little inn, and had bidden me look down through the roof of the cottage—if a friendly demon had done this, what should I have seen? An idle discontented woman lolling on a sofa, trying to read a novel, but too much occupied by her own vexations and her own vanity to be even interested in what she read — a peevish daughter, a neglectful sister: no ministering angel, no domestic treasure—nothing in the world but a conscious beauty, absorbed in the consideration of her own charms, and indignant at a social system which had provided no young nobleman ready to place his coronet upon her brow.

CHAPTER VII.

A BROKEN LIFE.

" I WENT out upon the little rustic balcony, and stood there with the warm evening air breathing softly round me. I could see the row of cottages, the neat little gardens that were so full of the simple flowers familiar to me in my youth. I could see the dim light shining here and there in a window; but I could not distinguish the particular habitation that sheltered my divinity; and I was half inclined to be angry with myself because no special instinct told me which it was. I was startled from my foolish meditations by the sound of a voice mingling with the other voices that floated up to me from the open windows of the parlour below; a voice that set my heart beating faster than it had beat since Caroline Catheron had vanished from my enchanted gaze; and yet it was not Miss Catheron's voice; it was only the bass growl of the organist. He was not the rose, but he was, at any rate, the companion of that wondrous flower. I went downstairs, and made a paltry pretence of putting my watch right by the clock in the bar-parlour; and then as I loitered talking to the landlord, he remarked that I might find myself dull in my solitary chamber upstairs, and suggested that I should step into the parlour, where a little knot of the most respectable inhabitants of Weldridge was wont to assemble nightly.

" 'There's Mr. Marles the clerk, and there's Mr. Scott the organist, quite a deep-read gentleman in his way, I've heard; and you'll rarely meet him without a book in his hand. And there's Mr. Stethcopp the baker, and Mr. Brinkenson, an independent gentleman, who occupies the first of that row of cottages as you come to directly you leave this door. Weldridge would be a dull place, you see, if there wasn't a little friendliness and sociability between the inhabitants. We've had some out-and-out gentlemen in our little parlour, I can tell you. There's Mr. Catheron, now, at one of the cottages; you might go a long day's walk and not find any one more the gentleman than him.'

"I could feel myself blushing when the innkeeper said this. It was so nice to know that the father of my divinity was a gentleman.

"'Mr. Catheron is a native of Weldridge, I suppose?' I said, interrogatively. I did not suppose any thing of the kind, but I was too far ingulfed in the abyss of folly to be straightforward in the smallest matter relating to Caroline Catheron.

"'Oh dear no!' exclaimed the innkeeper; 'Mr. Catheron does not belong to one of our Weldridge families.' He said this very much as if the inhabitants of Weldridge were a select and peculiarly-privileged people, infinitely superior to the most gentlemanly Catheron who ever lived. 'No, he is only a visitor in Weldridge, having come here for the benefit of his health, as you may have done, and having come upon the village promiscuous-like, just as you may have come upon it,' added the landlord, bringing the subject down to my comprehension as if I had been a child.

"I tell you all this frivolous stuff, Marcia, because even in my sorrow it is sweet to linger over these pages. I think of your hand resting on them by and by; I think of your breath ruffling the leaves. And then I want so much to confide in you. There is nothing in my life that I would hide from you, now you know what a broken life it is. I tell you this story of a boy's infatuation, in order that you may understand the folly which ruined my manhood.

"'Has Mr. Catheron — a — large family?' I asked; but I could boldly have anticipated the answer. Was it likely the father of a divinity would have many children? Goddesses do not grow in broods. My landlord answered my question as coolly as if he had been talking of Mr. Stetheopp the baker, or Mr. Brinkenson the independent gentleman.

"'There's a daughter,' he said; 'a very fine-grown young woman. And I've heard say there's another daughter — a married lady — away in the

Indies, or somewhere, with her husband. And there's a lad home for the holidays; a regular impudent young shaver.'

"I winced under the landlord's epithets of 'fine-grown young woman' and 'impudent young shaver,' as applied to my divinity and my divinity's brother; but it was a privilege to obtain any shred of information upon the subject of my infatuation, and I was very gracious to my informant. I cast about for a little further enlightenment on this one all-important question; but the landlord shifted his discourse to the current topics of Weldridge; so I told him I would avail myself of his suggestion; and I went shyly into the parlour, to make acquaintance with the notabilities of the village.

"I was received very civilly, very cordially; but I discovered the difference between the respect shown to a Pierrepoint at Pierrepoint and the familiar greeting offered to an unknown young traveller in a strange place. Mr. Stethcopp the baker patronised me, and Mr. Brinkenson the independent gentleman was almost regal in the superb condescension with which he offered me a chair near him. The little assembly was occupied in the discussion of public events. For a few minutes I listened respectfully to sentiments that were as strange to me as the discourses of the Mountain and the Gironde would have been to any young provincial aristocrat newly arrived from his hereditary lands. At Pierrepoint we were stanch Tories, from my uncle the squire to the peasant who gathered wood in the Chase. But the notabilities of Weldridge were Liberal to the backbone; and if my mind had been disengaged, I believe I should have entered into the lists against them in defence of my family principles, and might thereby have rendered myself very obnoxious. My mind had never been more completely absorbed, however; and I sat quietly under Mr. Brinkenson's wing with all the outward semblance of a respectful listener, while my thoughts hovered fondly about the splendid image of Caroline Catheron; and I thus secured the future favour of my companions as a very well-behaved young man.

"While they were deep in an argument as to the merits of Sir Robert Peel's last speech, I heard a strange voice—a voice that sounded foreign to Weldridge—in the bar without; and in the next moment I witnessed a social phenomenon. All at once the loud talk of the Weldridge notabilities dropped into a lower key; all at once Mr. Brinkenson the independent broke down in a Johnsonian period.

"'Mr. Catheron!' said Stethcopp the baker in a solemn hushed voice, and then the door was opened rather boisterously, and a gentleman entered the room.

"Her father! Yes, and he was like her. Again I was dazzled by the splendour of dark eyes, the glitter of white teeth, the warmth and richness of colour, the easy grace of manner which had fascinated me in the young lady I had followed from the churchyard. It was from her father that my divinity had inherited her full red lips, her aquiline nose, the dark arches above her flashing eyes; even the moustache that shaded Harold Catheron's lip was only an exaggeration of the ebon down that darkened his daughter's. Infatuated and bewitched though I was, one faint thrill of revulsion stirred my heart as I saw how much the man was like the woman. Surely in that moment I must have begun to understand vaguely that the attribute of womanliness was the one charm wanting in Miss Catheron's beauty.

"While I was wondering by what studied and subtle process I might approach the father of my idol, he took his place in the little assembly, and asserted the sway of town-bred ease over rustic stiffness as completely as if he had been in some acknowledged manner the sovereign lord and master of every creature in the room. While I was hoping that somebody would call his attention to me, and bring about an interchange of civilities, he turned to me with a graceful familiarity which was the very opposite of Mr. Brinkenson's, and yet infinitely more expressive of the difference between him, the gentleman of position, and me, the nameless stranger.

"'Your face is new to me,' he said; 'and yet not exactly new either, for I saw you from my window this afternoon, as my daughter came in from her walk. You are something of an invalid, I conclude, from your appearance; and if I am right, I can only tell you that you couldn't have a nicer place than Weldridge to get well in, or kinder people than Weldridge people to nurse you back to health and strength. I came here an invalid myself, and, egad, I think I shall go back to my own place a Hercules.'

"Heaven knows what I ought to have said in reply to this civil address. I know that I stammered and blushed, and then shyly asked Mr. Catheron whether he was going to leave Weldridge just yet.

"He told me no; his Weldridge friends treated him so well that he was in no hurry to leave them; and if his friend the butcher had only more liberal notions as to the number of calves required for the carrying on a business with justice to his customers in the matter of sweetbreads, and the number of sheep necessary to protect his customers from daily disappointment in relation to kidneys, he (Mr. Catheron) would have nothing left to wish for in the rustic paradise which an accident had revealed to his enraptured eyes.

"And then I told him how I too had fallen upon this pleasant resting-place by the merest chance that ever led an ignorant wanderer to his fate. And after that I grew bolder, and told him who and what I was, with some vague foolish notion lurking in my mind that when he found I was a Pierrepoint, he would open his arms and take me to his heart, and straightway invite me to his house and introduce me to his beautiful daughter. But he only nodded his head approvingly, and muttered,

"'Pierrepoint! A good old Yorkshire name, Pierrepoint! There was a Pierrepoint in my regiment, but he spelt his name with one *r*; and, between you and me, he was rather looked down upon as a snob.'

"'My uncle is Weldon Pierrepoint of Pierrepoint,' I said simply; 'and our name has been spelt with two *r*'s ever since the Conquest, when Hildred Pierrepoint—'

"'Exactly,' answered Mr. Catheron eagerly,—'came over with the Duke of Normandy, no doubt. Our people distinguished themselves at that period; but it was on the other side of the business. We were allied to Edward the Confessor, through Ethelfreda, the second wife of—but I won't trouble you with this sort of nonsense. My children have all these old stories by heart, and love to talk of them. For myself, I am a man of the world, and I know how little use your blue blood is to a man if he can't contrive to keep a decent balance at his banker's. And so your uncle is Weldon Pierrepoint, the wealthy squire of Pierrepoint in Yorkshire. I remember him at the clubs when I was a young man; rather eccentric, and a bachelor, if I remember right. Did he ever marry?'

"'Yes,' I answered; 'he married rather late in life.'

"'And had a family I suppose?'

"'Yes.' I told him there were three sons—lads at Eton.

"'Three of them! That's a bad job for you,

—that's to say if you are next heir to the estate.'

"I told Mr. Catheron that I was the next heir; but that I had no more expectation of inheriting the Pierrepoint property than I had of succeeding to a heritage in the moon. I told him how it had been decided that I was to be called to the bar; how my family had sent me to London, in order that I might see something of the world; and how I had been devoting myself to a course of preliminary reading in my Temple chambers.

"'But that's not exactly the way to see much of the world, I should think,' said Mr. Catheron smiling.

"I blushed as I answered him. I found myself blushing every minute in my intercourse with Mr. Catheron. I could not resist the impression that he was the father of my divinity, and that talking to him was only an indirect manner of talking to her. He looked at me more attentively after this little talk about my uncle, and when he got up to go away, he shook hands with me, and expressed a polite desire to see me again; but he did not invite me to his house.

I would have bartered all the letters of introduction fading in my desk for one line addressed to him. I went back to my own rooms immediately after his departure. I went to bed tired and languid, but not to sleep; only to lie awake thinking of Caroline Catheron.

"The next day was Sunday, and I went to the little village-church, where I saw her sitting meekly by her father's side. Shy though I was, I was bold enough to time my coming out so as to encounter them in the porch, and the beating of my heart almost stifled me, as we came out of the solemn shadow into the warm summer sunlight.

" It was not *I*, Marcia, who loved this woman for her beauty. My life and soul! I tell you again and again it was not I. It was only a foolish boy, who had no attribute in common with myself as I am to-day, but who had one quality, purer and higher than any I possess,— unlimited faith in the truth and honour of his fellow-men, boundless belief in the innocence and goodness of woman.

"Mr. Catheron turned to me in the friendliest manner as we came out into the churchyard, and offered me his hand, and then in the next moment I was introduced with all due ceremony to my divinity. She smiled graciously, and gave me courteous replies to my lumbering remarks about the fine summer weather, and the harvest, and the rustic loveliness of Weldridge. The condescending kindness of her manner inspired me with the fear that she looked upon me as the merest hobbledehoy; and I would have sacrificed half-a-dozen years of my life if I could have looked as many years older. She made only the faintest struggle with a yawn as we walked homewards under the trees by the very path along which I had followed her the evening before, and I saw her gaze wandering abstractedly to the ducks in the pond while her father lingered talking to me at his gate. Heaven only knows how keenly I felt her indifference. I think I should have gone away almost despairing if Mr. Catheron had not asked me to look in upon him in the evening, if I had nothing better to do. 'If I had nothing better to do!' as if in all the world there could be any more entrancing happiness than was to be found in her presence.

"'We are dull quiet people, my girl and I,' said Harold Catheron; 'but as you are a stranger and an invalid, you may find it pleasanter to spend a dull evening with us than a dull evening by yourself.'

"I thanked him as enthusiastically as if he had offered me a dukedom, and then went home on air. How I got rid of the rest of the day, I scarcely know. I could neither eat my dinner, nor read the newspaper which the landlord brought me. My books had not yet arrived. I walked up and down my little room until I was too weak to walk any longer, and then sat looking at my watch until seven o'clock. My landlord had informed me Mr. Catheron generally dined at five; and I had decided that I might decently pay my evening visit any time after seven.

"There was an unusual stillness upon the summer landscape when I went out of the little inn-door, and walked very slowly towards the house in which Harold Catheron lived. The Weldridge people were diligent church- and chapel-goers, and the majority of the small population was absorbed by the evening services. In that serene stillness I lingered for a few minutes, looking absently at the horses browsing on the green, possessed all at once by the hobbledehoy's shy dread of approaching the woman he admires; and then I summoned courage, and walked to the little gate. A boy of twelve or fourteen years of age, with a handsome defiant face, was lounging on the gate, and looked boldly up at me as I approached. There was sufficient resemblance to the features of my divinity in the boy's dark bold face to reveal him to me as the brother I had heard of. Anxious to conciliate any creature who bore her name, I saluted the boy very respectfully as I passed him, and received an insolent stare in return. A maid-servant admitted me, and ushered me immediately into a little parlour where Mr. Catheron was sleeping profoundly in an easy-chair, with his head thrown back upon the cushions and the edge of his newspaper resting upon the tip of his nose. No words can describe my disappointment as I looked round the room and saw how empty it was without my divinity. There was no sign of feminine occupation, no open book, no handkerchief or gathered flower thrown lightly aside by a woman's hand. There was nothing to betoken that Caroline Catheron had only lately left the apartment, and might speedily return. Mr. Catheron's newspapers scattered the table and the floor; Mr. Catheron's half-consumed cigar lay on the mantelpiece. Though the little garden outside the open window was rich in all sweet-scented cottage-flowers, the shabby chamber was not brightened by one gathered blossom.

"Cruelly disappointed, cruelly embarrassed, I seated myself opposite Mr. Catheron and awaited that gentleman's awakening. The newspaper dropped upon his breast, and I had ample leisure for the contemplation of his countenance. It was a very handsome face certainly,—how could it be otherwise than handsome when it was so like HERS?

—but its beauty was not quite pleasing even to my inexperienced eyes. It was a little too much like the face of a handsome vulture, who had cultivated a formidable pair of moustaches, and assumed a military style of undress. The curve of the aquiline nose, the bird-like modelling of the eyelids, the upward arch of the thin lips were not the characteristics of a noble countenance. I think I knew as much as this even then; I think I knew as much as this even that afternoon, when the spell of Caroline Catheron's beauty possessed me so completely that I had little consciousness of any thing except my eager desire to look upon her again.

"If I had presented my letters of introduction, if I had been enlightened as to the world I lived in by a year's intercourse with society, I should not have been so weak a wretch in the hands of Harold Catheron and his daughter. But the boy swinging on the garden-gate was my master in all knowledge to be acquired by the experience of life, and he knew it.

"My host started out of his sleep presently, and apologised to me for his inattention.

"'My daughter has gone to church,' he said; 'help yourself to a glass of that sherry; Caroline shall give us some tea when she comes in, and in the mean time you shall tell me all about your people in the North. You have no idea how the name of Pierrepoint brings back my young days, and the time when I knew Weldon Pierrepoint as one of the celebrities of the West-end. And so he turned country gentleman, and married, and had a family! Strange, strange.'

"Mr. Catheron's eyelids dropped languidly over his eyes, and he threw his head back upon the cushions of his chair, as if he had let his mind slip back to the past. Musing thus, and nodding his head every now and then with a little sigh of assent, he let me talk of my life at home, and of all who belonged to me. He let me talk— or it seemed to me at the time that he only let me talk; but even then I had some consciousness that it was he who kept my uncle Weldon's name perpetually uppermost in the conversation, bringing me back to that point when I was inclined to wander to some more cherished subject,—my mother's sweet companionship, my father's learning, my own ambitious dreams. However it came about, I told Harold Catheron all there was to tell about my uncle, and told him how the wealthy master of Pierrepoint Castle was a feeble invalid, with the poisonous taint of hereditary consumption in his blood, and with three sickly sons, whose uncertain health was a perpetual source of anxiety. 'And your father?' said Mr. Catheron, opening his eyes; 'is he consumptive too?'

"It seemed cruel to ask me such a question,— a question that must have struck home to my heart like a dagger, if I had been compelled to answer in the affirmative. Happily it was not so.

"'No,' I told him; 'my uncle Weldon and my father are only half-brothers. My grandfather married twice. His first wife died very young in a decline, leaving one son; and it is from her my uncle inherits his weak health.'

"'A sorry inheritance,' muttered my host; 'however, it is to be hoped that one or other of the three sons will escape the hereditary taint, and live to be master of Pierrepoint Castle. If you were a mercenary young man, it might seem almost uncivil to express such a hope in your presence; but I am sure that frank, open countenance of yours is not the face of a man who has any hankering for dead men's shoes.'

"I eagerly assured him how unwelcome that heritage would be to me which I could only reach across the graves of my three cousins; but he waved off the subject, as if its mere discussion were unworthy of us; and then I heard a light footstep in the garden, and the flutter of a dress, and the opening of a door, and my divinity came in.

"I am fain to confess that she looked cross and peevish, and that if any warning could have saved me from the consequences of my own folly, I might have taken warning by her manner on that day, and on many other days. But I think it is the peculiar property of a hobbledehoy's love to thrive upon ill-treatment; and perhaps Miss Catheron's disdainful airs and graces constituted only a part of the charm that bound me to her.

"It had been insufferably warm in church, she told us; and insufferably dusty on the way home from church; the sermon had been stupid; the singing execrable; and not a single stranger had been present to enliven the dowdy congregation. She made tea for us at her father's request; and she went through the processes of making it and pouring it out very much as if the task imposed upon her were the last straw laid upon the burden that rendered her life unendurable. But while we were taking our tea, and when I had ventured to talk to her, and had betrayed the completeness of my subjugation by every word I uttered, she brightened considerably, and by and by condescended to be supremely agreeable.

"Would you like to know what my wife was, Marcia, in that first day of our acquaintance, when I sat by her side in the little lodging-house parlour, while her father abandoned himself to his newspaper, and left us free to talk as foolishly as we pleased? What was she then, in all the bloom of her splendid beauty? A wicked woman? No; only a weak-minded woman; half-educated; influenced by no good example; elevated by no lofty teaching; left to go her own way, and taught to believe that in her beauty she possessed the 'Open, sesame!' to high fortune.

"She treated me with ineffable condescension that evening; but I could see that she was not displeased by my admiration, which was not expressed by any outspoken compliment, but evidenced no doubt in my every look and tone. There was a piano in the room, and her father asked her to play. She obeyed him with a very listless air; but she played some of Mozart's grandest masses magnificently, and her listlessness fell away from her like a cloud as she played.

"I sat by the piano, entranced by the sublimity of the music, bewitched by the beauty of the musician. I discovered afterwards that Caroline Catheron's mother had been a professional pianiste, and that the girl's love of music had been cultivated from infancy. Mr. Catheron talked of his absent daughter in the course of the evening, and I heard that my divinity's sister was a twin sister, and her living image.

"'My daughter Leonora married absurdly young,' Mr. Catheron said; 'and chose for her husband a grave middle-aged officer in the Company's service — a good match in a pecuniary sense, I admit, but by no means the kind of match I should have wished. However, my girl entertained quite a romantic devotion for Captain Fane, so I submitted to the force of circumstances; and my submission costs me my child, who has been scampering about with her husband's regiment in the jungles of Bengal for the last three years.'

"Caroline shrugged her shoulders a little contemptuously as her father made this lamentation. 'Pray, don't be sentimental, papa,' she said; 'what is the use of talking about love-matches, when you know very well you don't approve of them?'

"'I don't approve of a handsome woman throwing herself away upon a penniless scapegrace,' answered my host; 'but I disapprove of him because he is a scapegrace, and not because he is penniless. If a daughter of mine chose an honourable and talented young man for her husband, she should marry him with my consent, and my blessing into the bargain; provided always that the man was a gentleman, and the son of a gentleman.'

"I felt my face dyed a vivid crimson for some little time after this; and stealing a look at Caroline presently, I saw that the colour in her cheeks was heightened; and by the brightness of her eyes and the pouting of her lower lip, I knew that she was angry. Something in her father's speech had displeased her. She had been sitting at the piano until now, only turning to talk to us in the pauses of her playing; but she closed the instrument abruptly, and seated herself in an obscure corner behind her father's chair, where she obstinately remained for the rest of the evening, not to be lured from her retreat by any of the coaxing speeches with which Mr. Catheron tried to conciliate her.

"'Beauty is sulky,' he exclaimed at last,—he called his daughter Beauty, and he spoke to her very much in the tone which people are wont to use when caressing a favourite lap-dog,—'and when Beauty is sulky, *c'est un fait achevé.* The sun goes down at a given hour, and nothing less than a Joshua can induce him to postpone his setting. Phœbus himself is not more arbitrary than Beauty; and Beauty is more capricious than the sunshine. She has her bright days and her cloudy days; and to-day it is cloudy. If you will dine with us to-morrow, Mr. Pierrepoint, I will guarantee you a little sunshine, and we will have some secular music. Beauty and her brother Gervoise shall go to Barsett to fetch strawberries in the morning, and she shall sing Moore's melodies to us in the evening while we eat the strawberries she has fetched for us. If you are going Barsett way—and the old church is well worth seeing—you might help Beauty to carry her parcels. She would perish before she asked you any favour to-night, because she is sulky; but look in upon us after breakfast to-morrow, and I'll wager she'll be glad of your escort; for that tiresome boy of mine is always quarrelling with her.'

"The tiresome boy, whom I had first seen lounging at the gate, had been in and out a good deal in the course of the evening, and had been at last ignominiously ordered to bed by his father

If I say little of him, it is because I thought so little of him. I know now that Gervoise Catheron was shamefully neglected by his father and his sister; but at the time of which I write, my miserable infatuation had such full possession of me that I was conscious of nothing in this world except that Caroline Catheron was the most beautiful object in creation, and that I loved her. Despise me if you will, Marcia, but not more bitterly than you would despise a child who sees a gaudy butterfly for the first time, and fancies the possession of the radiant insect would afford him perpetual happiness. I was not quite twenty years of age when I fell in love with the woman who was afterwards my wife.

"A man might have been disenchanted by the insolence of conscious beauty, the capricious humours of an ill-tempered woman who gave full indulgence to her temper; but to a boy's mind these attributes only increase the charm of the woman he admires. The uncertainty of her smiles renders them doubly bewitching; her openly-expressed contempt fascinates the victim it might more naturally disgust; for it elevates the beautiful into the unattainable. When I thought of Miss Catheron that night, I thought of her as a being whom I could no more hope to win for my wife than I could hope to be the consort of a queen. I now know myself, as I was then, well enough to know that my passion would have lost its most powerful charm if it had lost its flavour of utter hopelessness. When I went home to my lodging that Sunday night, I sat by my open window, looking out at the moonlit landscape for upwards of an hour, enjoying my unhappiness, and thinking how convenient the village pond would be for me to drown myself in when Caroline Catheron had scornfully rejected my heart and hand.

"I found Mr. Catheron's prophecy realised when I presented myself at the cottage next morning. My divinity was very gracious, and we sallied forth on the best possible terms with each other, attended by the boy Gervoise, who came with us unwillingly enough, and who lounged and loitered behind us for all the length of our journey to and fro the little market-town of Barsett—a gay little town enough in those days, when there were coaches still upon every road, and pleasant bustle at every road-side inn. Miss Catheron had many little commissions to execute, and I was delightfully happy in attending upon her while she executed them. And then we all three went back to Weldridge loaded with airy little parcels and baskets of strawberries, and my divinity talked to me graciously, while the sulky boy lurked and loitered behind us. It was only a mile's walk across richly-wooded meadows, where the cows stood and stared at us in picturesque attitudes; but to an infatuated lad in love with a woman of three-and-twenty, it was a mile cut through the very heart of Paradise. I will not dwell upon this foolish courtship, though as I write, the past comes back upon me so vividly, that it is difficult to avoid recalling each separate stage of that unreasoning passion, whose evil consequences have blighted my life. It is enough for me to tell you that from the first moment in which Harold Catheron ascertained that only three consumptive boys stood between me and a great fortune, he set himself to win me as a husband for his daughter —the daughter whose capricious temper was the torment of his life; whose petted beauty had failed to realise the lofty expectations to which it had given birth; a daughter of whose airs and graces the selfish Sybarite had grown so weary that he would have been glad to dispose of her hand to the first bidder who could promise to support her decently.

"I was admitted into the little family on terms of perfect intimacy. I was invited to dinner twice a-week, and asked to drop in whenever I pleased. The tenderest of Moore's melodies were sung to me in a clear soprano every evening, and every evening I hung over Miss Catheron's shabby little hired piano, bewitched alike by the singing and the singer. But if my host was unvaryingly cordial in his manner, I had to endure all the transitions of his daughter's temper: and I did endure them as meekly as the basest slave who ever cast himself in the dust to be trampled upon by an angry Sultana. On the sunshiny days I basked in the light of Miss Catheron's smiles, and was happy; on the cloudy days I trembled before her frown, and was miserable. But the *primeurs* of life are very sweet; and my joy and my sorrow had the same freshness, the same flavour of youth and hope which intermingles itself with every emotion in the breast of boyhood. I was too much absorbed by my own feelings to be very curious as to the antecedents or the present circumstances of my new acquaintance. Mr. Catheron told me that he was the descendant of a grand old Saxon race, who could claim kinsmanship with the princes of the Heptarchy, and I believed him implicitly; for to my mind his daughter's beauty bore the stamp of royalty, since only the scion of kings had any right to be so beautiful. I listened respectfully to whatever Harold Catheron chose to tell me, and resigned myself to the belief that the Norman Pierrepoints were very small people indeed when compared to the Saxon Catherons. Incidentally I learned that Caroline's father had held a commission in the Grenadier Guards; had sold out on his marriage, and had spent three fortunes.

I have observed since this period that a ruined spendthrift has never spent less than three fortunes : the number is as arbitrary as the traditional half-crown which a millionaire carries in his pocket when he drops down worn and tired, a friendless boy, in the streets of London. After his wife's death, Harold Catheron had served under Don Carlos, and his daughters had spent the brightest days of their girlhood in Spain. For the last five years my friends had been wanderers in England and on the Continent, never staying very long any where, as I made out from their reminiscences of different places. What did it matter to me how or where my divinity's girlhood had been spent? It was enough for me to know that she was beautiful, and that it was my privilege to worship her. The time slipped by. The first cool breezes of autumn found me wandering in the stubbled fields beyond Weldridge with Caroline and her brother for my companions. I had been nearly three months an inmate of my lodging in the little village-inn. Long ago my health and strength had come back to me, and I had been backwards and forwards to the Temple, and had brought my law-books into the country, having argued with myself that it was almost as easy to pursue my studies at Weldridge as in London. But alas for my boyish dreams of greatness! The shades of Bacon and Coke had vanished out of my life. I tried to invoke them, but Caroline Catheron appeared to me in their stead; and after sitting over my books late into the quiet night, I found myself in the morning with no better fruit of my study than the vague remembrance of dreams in which her image had shone upon me. Still I did try honestly to work—still I held steadfastly to the hope of a great future. At the end of every week I wrote a long letter to my mother, in which I told her a good deal about my studies and my improving health, and a very little about my new friends. I meant to write to her at length upon this subject, and to confide entirely in her before I avowed myself to Miss Catheron. But I deferred the composition of this important letter from day to day, and from week to week; and the declaration which I had intended to be such a very formal business burst almost involuntarily from my lips one day while Caroline and I were gathering blackberries in the leafy hollow of a little wood, with Gervoise somewhere in attendance upon us.

"She was standing on a bank that raised her a little above me. She was looking down at me out of a framework of branches that closed around her as she stood there. It was one of her cloudy days, and her capricious temper had kept me in a state of torture all the afternoon. But she had melted suddenly at last, and had complained to me of the wretchedness of her life, the unkindness of her father, the daily degradations to which her poverty exposed her. She had complained to me with tears in her eyes—the peevish tears of a selfish woman who bemoans her own troubles, and has no consciousness of any thing upon this earth beyond herself and her personal pains and pleasures. But to me those tears were more afflicting than the aspect of a Niobe's anguish. Of all unreasoning passions, a boy's love is the most entirely unreasoning. And is a man's love so much better? Ah, Marcia! Even now, when I fancy myself so wise, do I love you because you are good and pure and holy? or do I love you only because I love you? By my life and soul, I cannot answer that question. But if I heard to-morrow that you had poisoned every one of those poor village children amongst whom I have seen you sitting,—so sweet and saintly a creature, that I have wondered not to see a halo of supernal light shine out from among the shadows round your head,—I scarcely think that I could love you less, so little within my own volition is the one absorbing sentiment that has become the first principle of my life. Forgive me for introducing your name into this record, which I had intended to make only an unvarnished statement of my miserable history; but your image and the madness of the present thrust themselves every now and then between me and the images of the past, and I forget that I have no right to tell you all I feel and suffer; I forget that I have no right to sully your name by inscribing it upon these pages.

"The sight of Miss Catheron's distress put all my prudent resolutions to flight. She was very unhappy with her father, she said; he did not care for her properly; when he was kindest he only treated her like a favourite spaniel; when he was out of temper he treated her worse than any dog was ever used since this world began. She said this in little snatches of words between passionate sobs, as she stood above me plucking pettishly at the leaves and brambles in the hedge about her. She talked to me with her face half-turned away, and I doubt if she was conscious of my presence. It was a relief to her to complain, and she complained. She showed me a scar across her plump white arm, the mark of a red-hot poker with which her father had struck her one day in his passion; but she acknowledged that he had not known the poker was hot. Her brother was rude and tiresome, she said. Her sister had married well, and had gone away to India, to enjoy life amongst all sorts of delightful people, without bestowing one thought upon leaving her to poverty and wretchedness, to cross landladies and shabby dresses. Her sister was, indeed, a selfish creature, and had never loved her properly.

No one loved her properly—no one—no one—no one!

" She beat her foot upon the ground, passionately moved by some deeper emotion than I had ever seen in her yet, as she reiterated those last words.

" ' Oh, Miss Catheron!' I cried; ' oh, Caroline, you must know how much I love you! you must know how much I—IDOLISE you!'

" I blushed as I uttered the big word, I believed so implicitly in myself and my own emotion. Caroline Catheron turned and looked down at me; her peevish frown vanished, and a half-amused smile lighted her face.

" ' You are such a boy compared to me,' she said. ' I don't believe you know what you are talking about.'

" Of course I told her that the passion which raged in my heart of hearts was eternal as the sky that overarched us that autumn afternoon. *Alastor* and the *Revolt of Islam* were terribly familiar to my lips in those days; and I blush even now when I think of the rodomontade in which I set forth my feelings for Miss Catheron. She was pleased with the romantic nonsense. It was her nature to be delighted with admiration and flattery, whencesoever it came. She forgot all about her troubles for the moment, and graciously condescended to stroll through the wood by my side, listening to my rhapsodies with drooping eyelids and a faint blush upon her cheeks. But if Caroline was forgetful of the evils she had so lately bewailed, I was not. I told her that if she would only accept the devotion of my life, she might be rescued at once from all the miseries of her existence, removed for ever from the ill-treatment of her father. It was true that I was for the moment by no means a rich man, having only a hundred a-year from my uncle, independent of my labour; but in a few years I should be called to the bar. And then I gave the reins to my ambitious imaginings, and informed my divinity of the glorious career I had mapped out for myself; a career which I must certainly achieve if she were by my side, the sweet companion of my toils, the idolised wife for whose dear sake the labours of a Hercules would seem the lightest tasks that ever man performed victoriously. I told her how, through the influence of my father's old friend the recluse of the Temple, I had already earned a good deal of money by writing certain learned essays for a quarterly review, and how I could rely on doubling my income from this source. And then the future! I had very little to offer my divinity in the present; but there are few grander prizes on this earth than those I promised her in the glorious days that were to come. She listened to me always with the same half-smile upon her rosy lips.

" ' Papa wouldn't much care whom I married, so long as he got rid of me,' she said, when I begged her to let me speak to her father. ' He used to talk very grandly about my making a great marriage, if I—if I did as he wished; but girls who wear washed-out muslin, and live in stupid lodgings in out-of-the-way villages, don't marry dukes or millionaires every day in the year; and I think papa begins to understand that.'

"I accepted this as a kind of permission to declare myself to her father; and then I implored her to answer the one grand question on which my future depended. Did she love me? Ah, no! I called back the presumptuous words the moment they were uttered. Was it not the wildest folly to imagine that she could love me? Would she tolerate my love? would she graciously permit me to be her slave? would she kindly consent to my lying prostrate in the dust at her feet? would she generously condescend to set her foot upon my neck? It was in some such phraseology as this that I asked Caroline Catheron to be my wife. It is not thus, Marcia, that, were I a free man, I would ask you the same solemn question.—I could win no decided answer from the capricious beauty. She tortured me by coquettish little speeches about her own heartlessness; her unfitness to be the wife of a struggling man; the difference between our ages; the incompatibility of our tempers. But her words and her manner were utterly at variance. On the one hand, she threw every imaginable obstacle in the way of my suit; while on the other, she gave me every encouragement to go on suing.

"'I don't suppose I shall ever marry at all,' she said. 'You know what a dreadful temper mine is, and how I have been spoiled by indulgence. If you want a submissive wife, you should marry some little fair-haired person with pink cheeks and white eyelashes. Dumpy people with freckles are generally amiable, I believe. You don't know how tired you would be of my temper after a week or two. Papa and I are always quarrelling. I give you fair warning, you see, of what you have to expect.'

"'What I had to expect!' That phrase sounded as if I was accepted. And for the warning, what warning would have stayed me in that mad folly of my boyhood? If a hand had come down from heaven to write the character of this woman in letters of fire across her brow, I would have believed in her beauty, and not in the writing that defaced it. I asked that night for a private interview with Mr. Catheron, and my request was granted. When I offered him my humble supplications to be received as the suitor of his daughter, he smiled graciously upon me, pleased, he said, by my boyish fervour, so refreshing in our degenerate days. He would not say no; he would not say yes. He would only say Wait! I was such a mere lad, he told me, that it would be foolish to depend too much upon the endurance of an affection whose highest charm was its youthful poetry. These boyish passions have sometimes withstood the wear and tear of a lifetime, and have endured in all their freshness to the grave; but, on the other hand, your early attachments are so apt to be fleeting; and of all the millstones you can tie round a man's neck, when you want to sink him effectually, a long engagement is the heaviest.

"'You say my daughter is disposed to look kindly on your suit,' Mr. Catheron said in conclusion. 'She is older than you by a year or two; but in character she is a mere child, and I should doubt her power to understand her own feelings. I can only say again, Wait! Go back to your studies; remember that the future you talk of can only be won by unremitting work; but come and see us now and then—every Sunday if you like. A quiet day in the country will re-fit you after your week's labours. Treat my daughter as if she were your friend or your sister, and by and by, when you are a year or two older and wiser, we will begin to think of a marriage. In the mean time there shall be no engagement whatever between you and Carry; and if you see any one you like better, you will be quite free to change your mind.'

"I had no argument to oppose against this very reasonable arrangement; and I gladly accepted it. Mr. Catheron gave me his blessing at parting, and further bestowed upon me a miniature of his two daughters, painted for him by an artist of some distinction before Leonora's marriage, and, as I have since had reason to believe, never paid for. With this treasure in my possession I went back to London at the end of the week, and set to work once more amongst my books in the dreary chambers under the tiled roof that had sheltered so many generations of briefless barristers. But the mighty shadows of the past had utterly deserted me; and the image of a beautiful woman was the only presence that kept me company in the long night-watches.

"When I went back to Weldridge to pay my first Sunday visit I wore a deep band of crape upon my hat, and I carried in my pocket a black-edged letter containing the news of my youngest cousin's death. The boy had been removed from Eton to fade slowly at Pierrepoint—the first victim to the hereditary taint that poisoned the blood of my uncle Weldon's race. Nothing could have been more sympathetic than Mr. Catheron's manner when I told him how the child had been the pet and darling of his household and our own. I looked to Caroline for sweeter consolation than any her father could give me: but she received my sad tidings very coolly, and said the little boy was no doubt much happier where he had gone, and it would be absurd to grieve for him. 'I wish I had died when I was a child,' she said; 'I'm sure I should have escaped all kinds of worry and trouble, and people would have been sorry for me, and would have said all manner of sentimental things about me: while as it is, I daresay every body will be very glad when I die.'

"Of course I told her that desolation and despair would attend her death, let it come when it would. I have prayed since that time—fervent passionate prayers—that I might be saved from the sin of wishing for her death; and yet *have* wished for it in spite of my prayers.

"I wrote to my mother as often as ever; but not as frankly as of old. My heart always failed me when I wanted to tell her of Caroline and my love. There would be so much for me to explain. I should have to answer so many questions. And then Captain Catheron was not in the position he had a right to occupy, and there would be the dreary story of a spendthrift's downfall to tell; and the story might prejudice my mother against Caroline. On the other hand, I argued that as I had entered into no positive engagement, there was really very little worth telling. There would be plenty of time for explanations by and by. I worked steadily every week, rarely leaving my chambers except for an hour's walk in the dusk of the evening, or for a day's work in the reading-room of the British Museum. I extended my literary connections after my return from Weldridge, and was a contributor to several periodicals of a high class. My work in this way brought me in a good deal of money, which I saved for Caroline. Mr. Catheron had told me incidentally that it would be utterly absurd of me to talk of marrying until I had the nest-egg of a modest fortune. I remembered this; and when I went dinnerless, as I very often did in those days, it was for Caroline's sake that I was economical.

"The autumn faded into winter—a hopelessly wet and cheerless winter—and I was working quietly on, with the dull round of my labours only broken by the Sunday visits to my divinity, who received me with smiles or frowns, according to the caprice of the hour. I might have spent my Christmas at Pierrepoint Castle, where my father and mother were keeping house, and dispensing old-fashioned charities and hospitality, in the absence of my uncle Weldon, who could only support the winter in a southern latitude. My mother wished me to be with her. My own heart yearned for her presence; but I was invited to spend the day with Caroline, and I could not break the chain that dragged me towards her. My literary work was a good excuse for my stay in London; and I added the sum that my journey would have cost me to the little hoard it was such thrilling pleasure to amass—for Caroline. My reward was the sulkiest reception I had ever yet endured at Miss Catheron's hands. She scarcely spoke to me half-a-dozen times during the dreary winter's day; and she only answered her father in monosyllables when he addressed her. Mr. Catheron tried to entertain me; but Caroline refused to play when he asked for music; and while I was trying to devise some means of seeing her alone, she announced that she was suffering tortures from a splitting headache, and wished me good-night, utterly regardless of my entreating looks, and the whisper in which I implored her to tell me what was amiss. Her father affected to believe the story of the head-ache, and completely ignored his daughter's ill-temper. I went home alone in the coach, through slushy roads and drizzling rains, very much cast down by my divinity's chilling behaviour, and thinking sadly of the lighted windows of Pierrepoint Castle shining out upon the dark night, and the pleasant party gathered round my father and mother in the cedar-panelled saloon.

"I was not permitted to write to Miss Catheron, so I was likely to remain in utter ignorance of the cause of her temper until the following Sunday, when I might find an opportunity of questioning her. I felt assured that something out of the common course had happened to disturb her; and the thought of this filled me with perplexity. I even found a difficulty in concentrating my mind upon my work, and waited uneasily for the end of the week.

"It was on Saturday night that an event occurred which decided the issue of my life. I had been writing for the best part of the day, and had sat at my desk till my head ached, and my cramped hand would scarcely form the characters upon the page before me. I left off at last from sheer exhaustion, and taking a volume at random from the pile of books before me, I began to read. But I had read a very few pages when my heavy eyelids dropped, and I fell into a doze—a doze that deepened into a profound slumber, in which I dreamed of wading knee-deep in a sluggish stream, with a starless sky above me, and a pitiless rain beating down upon my head. Amidst the thick darkness that surrounded me, I saw a light burning feebly in the far distance, and it was towards that distant glimmer I was trying to make my way. But spite of all my struggles I found myself receding rather than advancing, dragged backwards by some horrible weight that hung upon me and paralysed my movements. It was only a very common form of nightmare, I daresay, natural to the condition of an overworked brain; but sometimes I have been weak enough to imagine that the moral of my miserable life was set forth in that uncomfortable dream. I was wakened from it suddenly by the falling of my book, which had slipped from my loosened hand, and had dropped heavily upon the ground.

"There were two sounds in my ears when I awoke,—the pattering of the rain which I had heard in my sleep, and the sound of a hurried knocking at my door. I got up to answer the impatient summons, and on opening the door I beheld a woman, whose figure was undistinguishable under the voluminous folds of a heavy shawl, and whose face was hidden by a thick veil.

"Before I could address her she flung the dripping veil off her face, and I recognised Caroline Catheron.

"'Caroline!' I exclaimed, 'what in Heaven's name has brought you here at such an hour? Your father—'

"'Oh, there is nothing amiss with him, if that is what you mean!' she answered impatiently, 'though he is the cause of my being here to-night. There is nothing the matter with him except wickedness, and that seems to agree with some people. Let me sit down by your fire, please, Godfrey, and don't stand staring at me as if I were a ghost. Take my shawl,—and now my bonnet,' she said, handing me the dripping garments. 'Have you any woman-servant? No; I remember your charwoman only comes in the morning. However, that's no matter; I shall only stop with you till my shawl is dry, and then I want you to take me to an hotel of some kind, where I can have a lodging. It is not the least use your staring in that absurd manner, Mr. Pierrepoint. I'm never going back to Weldridge again, or to any other "dridge" where my papa resides.'

" ' But, Caroline—'

" She tossed her head impatiently. I had never seen her look more brilliantly handsome than she looked that night in her dark stuff gown, and with her black hair pushed carelessly off her face. I was too much bewildered by her presence to do any thing but stare at her, as she flung herself coolly into the chair in which I had been seated, and planted her wet feet on the fender. There was nothing bold or immodest in her familiarity; it was rather the easy manner of a popular queen who takes refuge in the dwelling of a subject, and is aware that she confers an honour by her presence.

"'It is not the least use your preaching to me about duty, or any thing of that kind,' she exclaimed. 'Come what may, I will never go back to any house in which my father lives. We have been quarrelling ever since I was old enough to quarrel, and on Christmas-eve matters came to a crisis. We have not spoken to each other, except under compulsion, since that night. Of course it's a very dreadful thing for a father and daughter to quarrel as we have done. I know that quite as well as you do; but papa's temper is unendurable to me, and I suppose my temper is unendurable to him. We are too much alike, I think. Papa is a tyrant, and wants to reign supreme among stupid, submissive people, who would never oppose him; and I am not submissive; or stupid, so far as I know; and the end of it all is, that we cannot exist any longer under the same roof. There's not the faintest reason for you to look so horrified, Godfrey; I am only going to do what girls in my position—and in more comfortable positions than mine—are doing every day of their lives. I am going out as a governess. If I had proposed such a thing to papa, he would have talked all sorts of pompous nonsense about the Catherons and Edward the Confessor, though he owns himself that Edward the Confessor never was the slightest use to him in any stage of his career. In fact, what papa would like would be for me to wait upon him, and play Mozart to him until my hair was gray, and to submit to be thwarted in the dearest wishes of my heart, and, in short, to be an uncomplaining slave. So, instead of fighting the matter out with him, I quietly left Weldridge by this evening's coach, and have walked from the coach-office here, not having enough money to pay for a cab. So I want you to lend me some money, please; and I want you to get me some kind of lodging.'

" 'But have you no friends in London to whom I could take you, Caroline?' I asked, looking anxiously at my watch. 'You would be more comfortable in a friend's house than in a strange lodging.'

" ' Of course I should,' Miss Catheron answered impatiently; 'but I have no friends to whom I can go at ten o'clock on a Saturday night, and say, "I have run away from papa, and I am going out as a governess: please accommodate me in the interval." Those sort of friends are not very common.'

"This was an unanswerable kind of argument; so I put on my hat and hurried out, after assuring Caroline that I would do my best to secure her safety and comfort. I had only one person to whom to appeal in my dilemma, and that person was my laundress, whose address I fortunately knew. I was also so fortunate as to find her at home, and up; and having made her my confidante, she informed me that she did know of a humble, but thoroughly respectable lodging, where the young lady could be accommodated at this short notice, and where she would be far less open to suspicion, or exposed to impertinent curiosity, than at an hotel.

"'Poor dear young creature,' said the laundress, 'she must be terrible cut up and timid-like, finding herself in London promiscuous like this, and with not a place to lay her pretty head in!'

"I informed the worthy woman that the young lady in question was a very high-spirited young lady, and not prone to timidity. Was I proud of her, or was I ashamed of her, because she was so different from other women? I can scarcely tell. I only know that the influence of her presence enslaved me, as the opium-eater's vice enslaves him, even when he knows most surely the ruin which it involves.

"The respectable lodging turned out to be a very tidy place in a little square behind Fleet Street; a quaint old-fashioned little square, so hemmed in and surrounded by taller and more important buildings, that a man might live close to it for half a century without being aware of its existence. I saw the landlady of the lodging-house, and having satisfied myself that she was a respectable and civil person, who would receive Caroline kindly, I parted from my laundress and went back to my chambers.

"I found my divinity sitting by the fire in the same attitude in which I had left her,—a very discontented and moody divinity, and by no means inclined to be enraptured with any arrangements I had made for her comfort. I remember now how completely she ignored any discomfort I might have suffered in my search for her lodging; but in the days of my folly she was as charming to me in her sulkiest temper as in her brightest mood, and I attended her that night with slavish humility, and saw her comfortably installed in her little third-floor sitting-room before I went back to my own chambers. I had taken five golden sovereigns from my hoard, and gave them to her when I wished her good-night. This was something to have worked for, this delightful privilege of ministering to her necessities, however coldly she might receive my service. I went home to think of her and dream of her; and I had the honour of attending her to the Temple Church next day, and of walking with her in the St. James's Park afterwards.

"It was during that walk that I urged upon her all the miseries of the step she contemplated taking; the difficulty of obtaining the assistance of her friends so long as she remained at variance with her father; the utter impossibility of finding any situation without the help and recommendation of friends; and, lastly, the absence of motive for such a course. Was I not at her command, ready to find a home in which she would be no dependent, but sole mistress, if she would only accept a home of my finding? Why should she not marry me at once, I argued; since she was determined not to go back to her father; and since, as she said herself, she was of an age to do what she pleased, without consulting any one? After I had pleaded for a long time, she agreed to consider my proposition, and to give me an answer on the following day. All that Sunday evening I sat alone in my garret-chamber, unable either to read or write, and with no better occupation than to count the hours and minutes which must elapse before I could know my fate.

"When I called on Caroline the next morning, I found her still irresolute, and had all my pleading to go through again; but at last I wrung from her a half-unwilling consent to an immediate marriage, and I left her by and by, feeling unutterably happy and unutterably important, with an enormous amount of business on my hands. But all at once, now that the critical moment had arrived, I was seized with a sudden feeling of doubt as to whether my father and mother would consent to this early marriage. Was it not almost certain that they would oppose such a step, on the ground of its imprudence—that they would even forbid it? I knew my mother well enough to know that she would wish to become intimately acquainted with Caroline before she received her as a daughter-in-law; and how could Caroline remain in a square at the back of Fleet Street until my mother could be brought up from Yorkshire to make her acquaintance; or how could I take my betrothed to Pierrepoint an uninvited guest, and in the very doubtful position of a runaway daughter? And then there was another question which I scarcely dared ask myself, so very doubtful was the answer. If there were time and opportunity for my mother to become familiar with Miss Catheron, would the result of the acquaintance be very satisfactory? The changeful temper, the imperious will, which were so charming to me, might fail to fascinate an anxious mother when exhibited by the future wife of her son. Debating my position in long and painful meditations, I became impressed by the conviction that I must follow the dictates of my heart at all hazards, and trust to the future to reconcile matters with my relations. A year ago, I should have as soon dreamed of jumping over London Bridge as of marrying without the knowledge or consent of my father and mother. But the bondage of affection and duty was only a spider's web in comparison with the chains that Caroline Catheron had riveted about me; and I flung every consideration to the winds rather than incur the hazard of losing the woman I loved.

"Early on the following day I made arrangements for our hasty marriage. As I was under age, and there would therefore be difficulty about a license, I had our bans put up at St. Dunstan's; for though I was base enough to keep the secret of my marriage from my relations, I was not prepared to perjure myself before a proctor. So, on the following Sunday and for two Sundays afterwards, the scanty worshippers in St. Dunstan's Church were asked if they were aware of any just impediment to the marriage of Godfrey Pierrepoint, bachelor, and Caroline Catheron, spinster; and on the fourth Monday after my divinity's arrival in London I stood by her side before the altar, in the semi-obscurity of a black winter's day, while a curate in a dingy surplice joined our hands in surely the most fatal union that was ever solemnised in that old City church. No one had interfered to prevent our marriage. Of all my father's friends no idle wanderer had entered the church in Fleet Street to be startled and scandalised by hearing the name of Pierrepoint amidst a string of Smiths and Joneses; while, on the other hand, Mr. Catheron had taken no step to reclaim his daughter, though he must have been well aware by the cessation of my Sunday visits to Weldridge that I was acquainted with her movements. And she was my wife—mine, my very own! Henceforth I was to be sole proprietor of the flashing eyes, the disdainful red lips: and the temper—with its every capricious change from cloud to sunshine, and from sunshine back to cloud. I took my bride to Brighton; and for the two short weeks of our honeymoon I found it a delicious thing to submit to her temper when she chose to be angry with me, and to be forgiven for having done nothing particular when she was tired of being sulky. Before I had time to discover that even these delights can pall, we returned to London, and took possession of a pretty little cottage at Camberwell—a cottage in a green winding lane, with a garden in which there were honeysuckles and roses in the summer time, and which even in February had a pleasant rural aspect. Thus Caroline and I began life together. I still kept the secret of my marriage from my family, trusting to the future for a favourable opportunity in which to disclose it. I left my wife early every morning to walk to the Temple, and returned to her after dark. Even now I cannot think of the dingy streets between the Temple and Blackfriars Bridge, or the long dusty road between the bridge and Camberwell Gate, without a shudder, they are so associated with this period of my life, and with the aching heart that I have carried in my breast as I tramped along them. How soon did I discover the fatal mistake that I had made! I look back, and beyond that brief honeymoon period I cannot remember any time in which I did not think how mad a thing my boyish folly had been, and how bitter a price I was to pay for having indulged it. Heaven help the man who marries a beauty! There are beautiful women enough in this world unconscious of their loveliness as the flowers that bloom and fade hidden in the untrodden woods. But from the professed beauty, the conscious enchantress, let man fly as from a pestilence—unless indeed he has a dukedom and some sixty thousand a-year to offer her; and even in that case she may hold him still her debtor. I found what it was to have married a woman who had been from her earliest girlhood impressed with the notion that in her handsome face she possessed the talisman which was to win her rank and fortune.

"From the very day of our marriage Caroline's complaints all harped upon one string—the sacrifice she had made in marrying me. I felt a guilty and dishonourable creature sometimes when she reminded me fretfully of the match she might have made, and the position she might have occupied but for me. The nest-egg of my future fortune was consumed prematurely in the furnishing of our suburban cottage; and the cost of the furniture was about on a level with that of a certain flat in Buccleuch Place, Edinburgh, wherein Francis Jeffrey and his young wife began their housekeeping, and in which modest household the *Edinburgh Review* was concocted. There are women who can invest a simple life with graces and beauties which are wanting in splendid homes; but the poetical side of poverty was beyond my wife's comprehension. It was all bitter, sordid, and miserable. Her ideas of housekeeping were derived from a reckless and extravagant epicurean, who would feast one day and starve the next, and who never paid for any thing until he had exhausted his credit. Thus, had I been a man to whom creature-comforts were essential, there might have been good reason for complaint on my side. One of my earliest unpleasant discoveries was the fact of my wife's extravagance. She took a great deal more money from me than I could afford to give her with any regard to prudence; and she deceived me repeatedly as to her disposal of it. Thus, after I had given her money for the payment of bills, I found the bills unpaid, and the money invested in an expensive bonnet, or frittered away upon gloves and ribbons. The simple muslin dresses and straw bonnets in which I had admired Miss Cathcron were contemptuously cast aside by Mrs. Pierrepoint; and I was called mean and cruel when I uttered any remonstrance regarding this change. All this I bore very patiently; but I had more to bear than this. My wife tormented me with perpetual entreaties to apply to my uncle Weldon for more money. Why should I not ask him for assistance? she said. He was rolling in wealth, her father had told her; and if his two sons died, I should be heir-presumptive to the estate; though of course it was quite certain that one of the horrid creatures would live, if it was only to keep *her* out of the fortune; for what good luck had ever come to *her*, or ever would, now that she had blighted her whole existence by marrying a pauper? Upon this point, however, my refusal was always decided. I told Caroline that under no circumstances would I apply to my uncle for further help; and I told her also that as soon as I found myself certain of a decent income, I should relinquish the hundred a-year he now allowed me. This matter was the cause of frequent disputes between us. Another subject of most bitter complaint with my wife was the dulness of her existence. So long as I kept the secret of my marriage, I was unable to introduce her to the society which was open to myself whenever I pleased to avail myself of my family connections. Day by day I grew more averse to any revelation of the step I had taken; for day by day I felt more certain that Caroline and my mother would never agree. The time would come, of course, when the secret must be told, and when those who loved me so devotedly, and who hoped so fondly in my future, must know how utterly I had wrecked it. I had a terrible foreboding that this knowledge would break my mother's heart; and it was this fear, rather than any cowardly dread of reproof, which kept me from revealing the change in my position. I paid a brief visit to Pierrepoint in the spring after my marriage; and the calm happiness of my old home seemed to me like a glimpse of heaven.

"Before I had been married six months I knew that my wife hated me. I might have discovered this incidentally in a hundred ways; but lest a shadow of doubt upon this subject should linger in my mind, the woman whom I had married told me one day in the very plainest terms that she had never loved me; that she had only married me to revenge herself upon her father, who had hindered her marriage with the man she had loved, and did love, and the mere sound of whose name was a hundred times more to her than I was or ever could be. She told me all this one day after a quarrel which had grown out of her peevish complaints about the petty miseries of her life. She told me those things in utter recklessness; and lest I should doubt the existence of the lover who was preferred to me, she took a little packet of letters from the desk before which she was sitting, and flung them to me.

"'Read those,' she said, 'and you will learn what a man can feel for the woman he loves. Those letters were written by a man with a heart and soul—not a dull plodder, not a miserable bookworm, who leaves his wife day after day to bury himself among his mouldy old volumes. Those letters are dearer to me now than any thing in the world. I read them every day while you are away from me; and at night, when you are sitting with your head buried in your books, I sit opposite to you and think about him. I am a very wicked woman, am I not? Did I ever tell you I was good? Did I not tell you a hundred times that I was utterly unfit for the life you could give me, and that poverty and dulness would drive me mad?'

"She had lashed herself into a kind of half-hysterical fury which was horribly familiar to me now, and she was pacing up and down the little room very much as a beautiful leopardess paces her den; quite as beautiful, quite as wicked-looking as the leopardess. I held the little packet in my hand,—a slender packet of letters that were worn and soiled by frequent handling,—a packet of some half-dozen letters tied together with a faded and attenuated ribbon. Upon the topmost envelope there appeared a greasy little circle, which indicated the presence of that most primitive and inexpensive of love-tokens, a slender ring of hair cut from a lover's head. I lifted the envelopes one by one, and looked at the address and post-mark upon each. They were addressed to Miss Catheron at a terrace in Kensington, and the post-marks upon them were dated a year before our marriage. Having ascertained this, I tossed the little packet into the hollow of the fire, and thrust it down with the poker.

"My wife sprang towards me, more like a leopardess even than before; and I knew by the attitude in which she paused, drawn back for a final spring that she was afraid to take, as well as by the nervous contraction of her slim fingers, that she would have liked to have struck me.

"We measured our powers of resistance that night for the first time. Until that hour I had been true to my position of a slave who submits to the despotism of his imperial mistress. But on that night the first spark of manhood was fired in my breast; the invisible bondage which had held me so long dropped away from me all in a moment, and from that moment I assumed a new position towards my wife.

"She looked at me with rage and astonishment blended in her face.

"'How dare you burn those letters!' she cried. 'They were mine!'

"'Mrs. Pierrepoint has no occasion to retain love-letters addressed to Miss Catheron,' I answered. 'I claim the right to destroy every thing that my wife has no right to keep.'

"'Oh, how I hate you! how I hate you!' she exclaimed, coming close up to me with the gliding cat-like step which I had admired as one of her charms. 'I married you because I was angry with my father for standing between me and the man I loved; because I never could forget or forgive that wrong; the bitter wrong which was the beginning and end of all our quarrels. And I married you because I was angry with *him* too; for if he had really loved me, he would never have let me go so easily. I married you because I hated myself and all the world; and because it was a mad and desperate thing to do, like jumping over Waterloo Bridge, or drinking corrosive sublimate. Poor pitiful fool! could you be weak enough to think that I loved you?'

" 'I was weak enough to think you a good woman. Whether you love me or not will be a very small question to me henceforward; but I shall know how to make you respect me.'

" From that hour my feelings with regard to my wife changed as utterly as if I myself had become a new man. I had been slavishly submissive to the capricious tempers of a coquette; but I revolted entirely against the insults of an unloving wife. There are men who will brook such insults, and cling with a base cowardly passion to the shrew who inflicts them; there are men who will accept the outward graces of the beauty that won them as a counterpoise to all inward hideousness; but I was not one of these. I had lived rapidly since my first meeting with Caroline Catheron; and from her father's cynical talk, and from her own unprincipled sentiments, I had acquired exactly the kind of knowledge which could never have come to me at Pierrepoint, even if I had existed there for half a century. After the burning of the letters my wife and I lived very much as we had lived before; for the fact that my passionate boyish love had utterly perished made very little difference in the dull current of our lives. I kept my word, and I taught Caroline to respect me. She grumbled still about our poverty; she exaggerated every little deprivation; but her complaints had lost their old power to wound me, for I no longer loved her. I listened submissively to what she had to say, and I did my best to make her life pleasant to her; but her unhappiness had ceased to be my keenest anguish; her pleasure was no longer my dearest joy. Do you know the resistance there is in a little field-flower which blooms half hidden among the grass? You may tread on it once, twice, thrice, a dozen times perhaps, and the elastic blossom will lift its head and go on blooming after your ill-usage; but trample on it just a little *too* ruthlessly, and it perishes beneath your foot, never to come back to life and beauty again. I sometimes think that love is such a blossom; and there are women to whom power is so sweet a thing that they must needs tread on the flower once too often.

"I had ceased to love my wife; and I was all the happier for the death of my ill-starred passion. My soul seemed to have escaped from bondage. I went back to my books with all my old zest. The mighty shadows came back to me. I was no longer the dull plodder I had been while my mind was occupied by Caroline's image and I worked against the grain. I was an enthusiast and a dreamer once more; and the editors for whom I worked congratulated me on the new fire which they perceived in my writing. Day by day I advanced, by some small step, on the path of literature. Success of a certain kind came to me, and in liberal measure. My earnings had been trebled within the past six months, and I gave my wife the full benefit of my improved position. But do what you may for the horseleech's daughters, the cry will still be 'Give!' If I took Caroline to the pit of the Opera, she was unhappy because she was not in the stalls; if I took her to the stalls, she bewailed the hardship of her fate as compared with that of a woman who had her box for the season. It is very difficult for a struggling man to satisfy a pampered beauty, who thinks she ought to have married a nobleman with sixty thousand a-year. I tried to do my duty, and there was something like peace in our household; for Caroline had discovered that there was a certain point at which her complainings must cease. Our mode of life had been in every way improved since the first days of our marriage. We kept two experienced women-servants now, in place of the maid-of-all-work who had been our only attendant. I added many small luxuries to my wife's simply-furnished rooms; and I paid a florist liberally for the cultivation of our small garden. There are many young wives who would have taken a tender pleasure in such a home as ours. I think of you, Marcia, in that rustic cottage; and I can fancy you happier in those unpretending chambers than you could be in a palace.

"We had been married a year, when Providence bestowed upon me the most precious gift I ever received from the hands of Heaven; except your love, Marcia,—except your love! I went home one evening in the bleak winter weather to find lights in the upper windows, while darkness and confusion reigned below; and to be told that I was the father of a son. There are subjects whose first pain never grows less. When I think of my only child, all the anguish connected with his brief existence comes back to me; and I feel the bitterness of my first great grief to-night as deeply as I felt it when the wound was new.

"For the first month of the child's existence his mother seemed inclined to be pleased and amused with him; and my heart softened to something of its old tenderness when I saw her sitting with her baby in her arms. I would gladly have relaxed my labours in some measure, in order to spend more time with my wife and child; but Caroline's extravagance kept me tied to the mill, and, work as I would, I could not earn enough to keep myself free from debt. I was of age by this time, and had been called to the bar; but my first brief had not yet come to me, and it was literature rather than law which occupied me daily at my Temple chambers, and very often deep into the night at home.

"My son was two months old, and already a faint smile of recognition had begun to dawn upon his face when I took him in my arms. Caroline was beginning to show considerable weariness of her new duties; and I heard all the old complaints about want of society and want of money, when an event occurred which delighted my wife, and made no inconsiderable addition to our expenses.

"Caroline's twin sister, the wife of Captain Fane, came home from India with her little girl, and volunteered to pay us a visit. As I was very glad to give my wife any reasonable pleasure, I united cordially in the preparations for Mrs. Fane's reception; and if I could have worked harder than I had been working for the last year of my life, I would have done so. A room was prettily furnished for our expected visitor, and a rather alarming invoice from the upholsterer reminded me that I was getting deeper into debt; but my wife promised me that she would retrench after her sister's departure, and I resigned myself to the cost of her pleasure. That she should be pleased in any innocent womanly manner was my highest wish; for the knowledge of the change in my own heart made me peculiarly anxious to do my duty to the woman I had once so devotedly loved.

"I came home one evening to find a lady sitting by the fire in the spring twilight—a lady whom I addressed as my wife. But something in her manner of rising and coming towards me was so unlike my wife—who rarely acknowledged my return by any thing but a peevish shrug of her shoulders and the remark that I was later than usual—that I understood at once the lady was my visitor. The likeness between the twin sisters was something extraordinary, so extraordinary that in the dim twilight I had difficulty in believing that the woman who stood before me was indeed a stranger. I saw afterwards that Mrs. Fane's complexion had a pale sallow tint, which made her beauty less gorgeous than the red-and-white loveliness of her sister. Nor was this the only difference between the two women; for I discovered ere long that in the expression the two faces were dissimilar. Caroline's was the countenance of a weak frivolous woman; Leonora's was the index of a resolute and powerful character.

"Mrs. Fane had placed her little girl at a school at Brixton, and after remaining with us six weeks as our guest, she persuaded Caroline to allow her to remain in the character of a boarder. I did not like this arrangement; for, in the first place, the pride of the Pierrepoints revolted against any thing like the sale of meat and drink, as the pride of an Arab might revolt against accepting payment for the sacred bread and salt bestowed on the stranger; and, in the second place, Mrs. Fane's presence in our household involved us in extravagances which her payments by no means counterbalanced. But I submitted to this; as I submitted always to any reasonable desire of the wife I had ceased to love.

"I knew that the two women often quarrelled, but on the whole they seemed happy together; and it pleased me to think, while I bent over my desk in the Temple, that my wife was not without a suitable companion. For myself, I had considerable difficulty in overcoming an instinctive dislike of Leonora Fane. I fancied her manners artificial, her smile false, her laugh hollow, her conversation stereotyped and conventional; but she was scrupulously polite and deferential in her conduct towards me, and the first impression faded out in our daily intercourse, until I began to think her really a very agreeable woman, whose easy temper my wife might do well to emulate.

"From the time of my sister-in-law's arrival,

I heard no more lamentations upon the want of visitors to our little household. Several of Mrs. Fane's friends came to see her, and I dreaded every day that through some of these people the news of my marriage might reach Pierrepoint. I heard very often when I went home of the callers who had been during the day, and I speedily began to take notice that amongst these visitors the gentlemen were in the majority. This perplexed me; and one evening, trifling absently with the little card-basket on my wife's table, I was startled by discovering that half the cards in it—and it evidently contained the accumulation of some weeks—were inscribed with one name, and that the name of a gentleman, a barrister of the Middle Temple, a certain Mr. Arthur Holroyde, whose name I had never heard or seen in any legal capacity, and whom I imagined to be as briefless a barrister as myself. I called my wife's attention to the number of the cards, and I asked her how this Mr. Holroyde happened to call so often, and whether she thought Captain Fane would quite approve any gentleman making such frequent visits to his wife. Caroline expressed extreme indignation at this suggestion. It was utterly preposterous and absurd, she said. Mr. Holroyde's visits to Leonora were the most ordinary visits in the world. Indeed, she added, he came to see her quite as much as her sister.

"'In that case,' I said, 'I must beg to object to the number of his visits within the past few weeks; and I think, as you are now subject to the morning calls of Captain Fane's Indian friends, it will be better for me to do my work at home, and thus be at hand to assist in the reception of your visitors.'

"I could see that this displeased my wife, though she was silent. From this day I altered my plan of life. My chief reason for spending the greater part of my time at the Temple had been the fact that there alone I found perfect peace and quiet. I now appropriated a little den of a back-parlour as my study; and I gave my wife to understand that the apartment must be kept sacred to me. In this den I worked, and from this den I emerged occasionally when Mrs.

Fane's visitors were in the drawing-room. I found her friends chiefly of the Anglo-Indian order, and I saw no reason to resent their presence in my house.

"For some weeks after this change in our arrangements I heard nothing of Mr. Holroyde. My habits at home by degrees became the counterpart of my habits in the Temple. I worked alone all day, shut as completely from the outer world in my little back-parlour as in my attic-chambers; and Mrs. Fane's visitors came and went unheeded by me. Our dinner-hour was very late; to suit my convenience, my wife said. Sometimes Caroline and her sister were out all day; sometimes I heard them playing and singing together in the little drawing-room. If ever I broke in upon them, I found them pleasantly and innocently amused; if ever I questioned my wife as to the time she spent away from home, I received satisfactory answers. But one day, coming into the drawing-room unexpectedly, I found Mr. Holroyde installed there, and a great deal more at his ease than I thought Captain Fane would have cared to see any man in the society of his wife. He was standing by the piano, and bending over Leonora as she played. I had heard the sound of the instrument all through the morning, and had therefore concluded that my wife and her sister were alone. I think I knew instinctively who this man was before he was introduced to me. He was a tall elegant-looking man of about five-and-thirty, with a long pale face, neither handsome nor ill-looking, but one of those faces which set people thinking—the face of a man who must inevitably make a strong impression of some kind or other upon the world in which he lives. His manner was peculiarly soft and conciliating—the sort of manner that women generally call fascinating; and in the little conversation which followed my introduction to him I had reason to conclude that he was clever and well-informed; but his cleverness was of a light airy kind, utterly different from that to which I had been accustomed in my father.

"When he was gone, I asked Mrs. Fane if he had ever been in India, and she told me no.

He was not a Calcutta acquaintance; he was an old friend of her husband's, whom she had known before her marriage. She praised him highly, but with an air of perfect indifference; and I concluded that Captain Fane had, after all, no occasion for displeasure.

"But after this Mr. Holroyde came very often; and meeting the servant in the hall one day, immediately after she had ushered him into the drawing-room, I asked who the visitor was. The girl had some difficulty in remembering his name.

"'Mr. Hol—Mr. Holroy,' she stammered,—'Mr.—oh dear, how stupid I am!—the gentleman who comes nearly every day, sir.'

"I was very angry when I heard this, and I remonstrated with my wife upon the subject that afternoon; but she received my remonstrances with an impenetrable sulkiness; and I determined to take some decisive step. I went to the Temple early the next morning, and called upon my father's old friend, the legal celebrity. He received me kindly; and without any special explanation of my reason for asking such questions. I begged him to tell me whether he was acquainted with Arthur Holroyde, and whether he knew any thing to that gentleman's discredit. The old man's answer was most decisive.

"'If you consider it to a man's discredit to be a thorough-paced scoundrel,' he said, 'I know that much of Mr. Arthur Holroyde; and if you are in any way mixed up with him, all I can say is, you had better get yourself out of the connection as soon as you can.'

"After this he told me that Arthur Holroyde belonged to a good old family; that he had spent a fortune about town; that he had degenerated from a gentlemanly dupe into a gentlemanly black-leg; that he was plausible and dangerous, false and cowardly; that the slightest association with his name was death to a woman's reputation; that any thing like friendship for himself was certain ruin to a man.

"I went home after hearing this, and told my wife and her sister that Mr. Holroyde must never again be received under my roof. Mrs. Fane, I said, was her own mistress, and if she insisted upon receiving him, she could take up her abode elsewhere; but if she would permit me the privilege of a brother-in-law, I should certainly most earnestly recommend her to resign that gentleman's acquaintance. Leonora Fane listened to this with perfect good-temper. She told me with a careless laugh that Mr. Holroyde was perfectly indifferent to her. She added that she had certainly made arrangements for leaving us in the course of the following week, but her only reason for so doing was the desire to give her little girl a change of air at some pleasant watering-place, where she hoped I would take my wife. I had addressed myself chiefly to Mrs. Fane, and I was in no way surprised by Caroline's silence. Nothing further was said upon the subject of Mr. Holroyde; but there was a little stiffness in my intercourse with my sister-in-law after this, and I was considerably relieved by her departure, which took place within a few days.

"A new source of anxiety arose for me about this time, the commencement of my great sorrow.

Amidst all the dis-illusions of my married life, my baby-son had been the one sweet reality—the one deep and pure joy; and I loved him with a passionate fondness that an infant rarely inspires in the breast of a father. My wife had for some time felt a capricious kind of fondness for the child, which had grown weaker with every day of its weakly life. To half smother it with caresses at one time, and to forget its existence at another, was only natural to such a person as Caroline. But as the infant's health grew week by week more delicate, the mother's love gave place to a peevish impatience of the trouble and anxiety involved in this feeble little life, which needed as careful watching as the flame of a candle flickering in a current of air. A few days after Mrs. Fane's departure, my boy grew worse than he had been yet. I cannot enter into the details of these infantine maladies, though, Heaven knows, no nurse or doctor ever watched their progress more closely than I have done. The medical man whom I consulted told me that the child's health depended in a considerable degree upon the mother's, and asked me if my wife's mind had been disturbed of late. He had asked her the same question, he told me; for her manner had led him to infer that she had been subject to some mental disturbance; but she had appeared much offended by the suggestion. After this interview, I tried to awaken my wife to the consciousness of her child's danger. I was talking to stone. With an agony that was more bitter than any I had ever before suffered at the hands of this woman, I discovered that my boy's fate was utterly indifferent to her. I perceived this; and yet in the next moment I believed that her indifference was affected,—a mere bravado assumed to annoy me. I thought this; for though I knew the woman I had married to be an unloving wife, I could not believe her an unloving mother. Then I made my first and last appeal to the better feelings of this creature. I implored her to perform the sweetest duties of womanhood. I was willing to allow much for her defective education; I was ready to admit her right to a brighter life than that which I could give her in the present. And then I offered her my future. I reminded her of the pathways to fortune that were opening for me on every side; I told her the promises that had been made to me by men who held fame and wealth in the palms of their hands; I told her that, if she would be a good mother, my dearest hope should be to win the affection she had never yet given me, and to love her again as I had loved her at first. I told her this, and I entreated her to believe in my power to win for her the position she aspired to, the pleasures and grandeurs she had a right to expect. I was weak enough to believe that I had indeed wronged her in some degree by shutting her from the chance of making a better marriage. 'Only save my boy,' I entreated, ' and be patient.'

"'Yes,' she cried, contemptuously: ' and I suppose, when I am an old woman you will give me a house in Russell Square, and a great blundering carriage that would look like a tub when it was open, and a mourning-coach when it was shut. I have seen poor milk-and-water creatures who have married "rising men," and who have begun to enjoy life just when women of spirit would be thinking of dying.'

"This conversation took place when my boy was very ill. After this, his mother made some little show of attending to him; but I could see that her mind was distracted, and I vainly endeavoured to discover the cause of her distraction. To me her manner was more coldly insolent than it had ever been yet, and there was something in her tone of defiance which reminded me painfully of the manner of a servant to whom Caroline had given notice of dismissal. If my heart and mind had not been so absorbed by love and anxiety for my boy, I might perhaps have discovered the clue to my wife's conduct; and yet I doubt if any freedom of mind would have enabled me to understand a woman who was so different from the mother beneath whose care my boyhood had been passed. I believed my wife to be weak, selfish, passionate, and vain; but I suspected no hidden treachery lurking darkly beneath those unconcealed vices.

"My boy rallied a little, and I began to hope.

I had neglected my work during the child's illness; for the little fellow knew me, and smiled at me, and I fancied he was pleased to have me sitting by his cot. One long summer-day I sat with him thus from noon till sunset, with my books on the table by my side, but infinitely more occupied by the child's presence than by them. On this particular day Caroline shared my watch, and sat at the foot of the little cot, looking sometimes at me, sometimes at the child, with a wan haggard face, in which I could see the traces of anxiety. My heart was softened towards her by the sight of her altered aspect. She did love the child, after all, I thought; and her affected indifference had been the result of ill-temper. I approached her, and tried to take her hand; but she repulsed me fiercely, and preserved a sulky silence all through the day. The sun was setting, when she flung herself upon the ground with a sudden energy that was almost terrible, and began to beat her head with her clenched hands.

"'Oh, what a wicked wretch I am!' she cried; 'how wicked, how wicked, how wicked!'

"I knelt beside her, and lifted her in my arms; but to do so needed all the strength which has since served me in a close grapple with a wildboar. Her whole frame was convulsed by the violence of her passion; but she grew calm presently, and when I tried to reason with her, and to discover the cause of her agitation, she lapsed back into the sulky silence that was so common to her, and by neither command nor entreaty could I wring a word from her lips. By and by she softened a little, and sat with her infant in her arms, crying over him; and when it had grown quite dark she kissed him, laid him gently, sleeping, in his nurse's arms, and left the nursery.

"After this I went downstairs to my den, lighted my lamp, and set to work. My literary labours had fallen into arrear, and it was only by writing all night that I could keep my engagements. I wrote first by lamplight, and then by daylight, until the little clock on the chimneypiece struck seven, when I lay down on a sofa in the warm summer sunshine, and fell into a sound slumber. When I awoke, it was late in the forenoon, and I heard the cries of hawkers and the sound of wheels in the distance. I went into our common sitting-room. The breakfast-table was laid for one, and nothing upon it had been disturbed. I opened the door, and called my wife by her name. The housemaid came to answer my summons.

"'My mistress went out last night, sir,' she said; 'and I don't think she's coming back for some days. I believe she's gone to Mrs. Fane. But there's a note behind one of the vases on the mantelpiece.'

"I went back to the sitting-room, and found my wife's letter. Did I guess what had happened, before I broke the seal? I scarcely know. All that most hideous time is dim and confused in my mind, as I try to recall it. The letter contained only a few lines; but it told me that my wife had left me for ever with the lover of her youth.

"Before nightfall I was on my way to Lyme Regis, where Mrs. Fane and her little girl were staying. I found my sister-in-law; but though I know now, and though I knew instinctively then that she was acquainted with my wife's movements, I could not wring a word from her. After my useless interview with this woman, I searched England and that part of the Continent which is most affected by English travellers, for the wife who had betrayed me; but in vain. I came back to England utterly worn-out by my useless wanderings, to find that my poor fragile boy had pined and drooped from the hour of his mother's desertion, and had died within a week of her flight. And I came back to find a letter waiting for me— a letter posted from America, and addressed to me in the handwriting of a man. The letter itself was written by my wife; and surely never, before or since, did a woman's hand so coldly and deliberately set forth a woman's sin. As I read those studied lines, so hideous in their effrontery, so revolting in their affected candour, I knew that I was reading an epistle in which my wife's brain had had little part, though my wife's hand had written the words. I recognised the carefully-prepared composition of a hard-headed, false-hearted scoundrel, in whose power Caroline

Pierrepoint was the poorest automaton that ever obeyed the guiding-strings of a showman. Upon my knees, with this vile letter clasped in my uplifted hand, I swore to inflict a fitting chastisement on the man who had dictated it. Who he was, how he had corresponded with my weak and wicked wife since her marriage, I had as yet no idea; but my memory helped me with regard to his handwriting, and I knew that it was his hand which had addressed the little packet of letters I had burned unread. A sudden fancy flashed upon me that night of my miserable return, as I sat brooding over my wife's infamous letter; and I went early the next morning to my father's friend in the Temple. Of him I again inquired about Arthur Holroyde, and I learned that he had left England some weeks before, deeply in debt, and obliged to fly from the chance of imprisonment. He had been since declared an outlaw. Following up this clue patiently and resolutely, I discovered that beyond a doubt Arthur Holroyde was the man who had sailed for America with my wife. I ascertained the name of the vessel that had carried them, the port at which they had landed. Having discovered so much, my course was clear; and for two weary unprofitable years my life was one long pursuit of the man who had wronged me.

"I followed this man and his most wretched companion from city to city and from state to state; guided sometimes by positive intelligence, wandering idly at other times in the vague hope of being aided by accident. Travelling thus, with the same purpose always in my mind, I visited every city in the United States, and made my way through Spanish America. I knew that Arthur Holroyde had taken his passage to New York under an assumed name, and that the people whom I was seeking called themselves Mr. and Mrs. Howell. I heard of them for the last time at Buenos Ayres; and though I had no positive intelligence upon the point, I concluded they had left that place for Europe. I could form no conjecture as to what vessel they had sailed by, or whither they had gone; and I came back to England hopeless of any successful climax to my long chase. I suppose the days of duelling were utterly gone by even then,

Marcia, and that if I had met that man face to face there would have been only a brief war of words, and a little windfall in the way of business for our solicitors. And yet, looking back to what I was in those days, I am inclined to wonder whether we two could have met without some deadlier mischief. I never thought of this while I was looking for my enemy; I only knew that I wanted to find him.

"I came back to England. I had kept up a spasmodic kind of correspondence with home and dear home friends during my wretched wanderings; but my father and mother believed that I was travelling for my own pleasure, and I was obliged to fill my letters with long descriptions of places which I only saw like streets and buildings in a dream. There were times when I was not equal to do this; there were times when a dull despair came down upon my soul, and I was stupidly indifferent to all the past, incapable of remembering or comprehending any thing except the present. Thus it was that my correspondence with home had been utterly irregular; and when I turned my back upon the mighty lands, compared to which my own dear island seemed such a speck upon the universe, six months had gone by since I had received news from home. Black-edged letters had come to me during my absence from England, —one announcing the death of my uncle Weldon at Madeira; the other, the death of his eldest boy at Ventnor. The two events had occurred almost simultaneously. I felt only a brief pang of regret when I received these sad tidings. What time had I to be sorry for the loss of the kindred I had once tenderly loved? The thought that only one frail life stood between my bookworm father and the Pierrepoint estate never entered my mind. I do not think I should have thought of it under any circumstances; I know that I never thought of it as it was.

"I went back to England. My old friend in the Temple could give me no information about Arthur Holroyde, except that he had not been heard of in London since my departure, and that even his creditors had ceased to talk of him or trouble themselves about him. I ran down to

Pierrepoint, and found my mother sitting under the apple-blossoms in the dear old garden. For one brief moment she was alarmed by the aspect of the gaunt bearded creature who held out his arms towards her, but in the next instant she was sobbing on my breast. I stopped at Pierrepoint for a week; but in all my visit I felt like a creature who had come back from the grave, and who had no part in the joys or sorrows of the living. My love for my mother was unweakened by our separation, but I had resolved to keep the wretched story of my marriage locked in my own breast; and the consciousness of carrying this secret load upon my mind oppressed me like the sense of some bodily burden.

"I saw my cousin, the young lord of Pierrepoint, and the lad's talk of his own grand future, and the new glory he was to win for our name by his triumphs as a statesman, wounded me as keenly as if every word had been chosen for my special torment. There was no old pleasure, no tender memory in the familiar home, which did not transform itself into a weapon for my pain and punishment. I left my fragile cousin lying on a sofa in the great oriel window, with a pile of blue-books by his side, flushed with feverish enthusiasm, and inexpressibly happy in the contemplation of a future that never was to be. I left my mother weeding her flower-beds, in a cotton gown, within call of my father's study-window, innocently happy in the simplest and purest life that ever woman led; and I left Pierrepoint resolved that I would never enter it again. What had I and my dishonour to do in the place where my name had been for centuries the symbol of all earthly pride and splendour?

"I went back to London. I abandoned all thought of finding Arthur Holroyde. Perhaps my thirst for vengeance or redress had exhausted itself, as every passion will exhaust itself sooner or later, in bodily fatigue and mental wear and tear. I settled back into my old chambers, poorer than when I had entered them first, and deeply in debt; for I had mortgaged years of my literary labour in order to borrow the funds that had supported me in my wanderings. I settled back to my old work, in my old rooms; and the only difference in me or my life was the fact that I was an old man instead of a young one. There are happy people who count their lives by years. The record of *my* existence is the record of my misery and my shame.

"I had been settled in my old chambers for six or eight months, when a letter from my father brought me the news of my cousin's death. I had seen him, and I had seen the fatal flush upon his face, the death-light in his mild blue eyes; but I had never contemplated the chances of the future. How could I desire wealth, since the unremitting labour that was necessary to my existence was the chief blessing of my life? Bending over my desk, I forgot what a blighted wretch I was. Carried away by that fairy wand—the pen, I entered lofty regions in which Caroline Catheron and her wickedness had no place.

"On the receipt of my father's letter, I felt the bitterness of my position more deeply than I had ever felt it yet; for he told me that my cousin had left me his private fortune, and that his last and dearest wish, expressed a few hours before his death, had been that I should stand for the North Riding, and enter the House as the representative of the Pierrepoints, and the advocate of those principles which had been so dear to his own heart.

"The estate to which my father succeeded, when the last of the Weldon Pierrepoints had been laid in the family vault, was one of the finest in the North Riding; the fortune which my cousin left to me was more than enough for any man with moderate desires. And I was expected to go back to Pierrepoint, to take my place by my father's side, and to carry out the dying wish of my kinsman.

"I was now rich enough to obtain a divorce, even in those days when to be set free from a false wife was so costly a measure; but I could not bring myself to drag my shameful secret into the light of day. I could not offer my bleeding heart for vivisection in the law-courts; I could not trail the name of Pierrepoint through the infected byeways that could alone lead me to liberty. I wanted to go back to my native place with my head erect. Could I do that, if every boor in the village were able to point to me as the man who had just been divorced from a runaway wife? And my father's sense of a share in my disgrace, and my mother's sorrow—could I bear those? No! I knew the full pressure of my present burden, and it weighed on myself alone. I knew this, and I was resolved to bear it patiently to the end. The thought that I should ever wish to be set free from my wife, for any reason except that it was a shameful thing to be allied to her, never entered my mind. The future which I saw before me was only a flat sunless plain, upon which I must tramp onwards till I dropped.

"I stayed in London for some weeks after the change in my fortunes, quite unchanged as to my habits. I paid my debts, and prepared for an early departure on those travels which have occupied so many years of my life. I told my father and mother nothing of my intended exile—for I had no reason to advance for the course I was about to take—and I determined to write only when I had started on my African journey. While I was busy with my preparations for a long and perhaps dangerous expedition, I received two visits,—one from Harold Catheron, who said he had lately returned from the Continent, to hear of my good fortune, and who told me a plausible story of his own virtues as a father, and his daughter's ill-treatment. He could tell me nothing of Caroline's whereabouts; and he had been deserted most cruelly, he said, by her sister Leonora, who was now a widow, with a small income. The purport of his visit was to ask me for money. I gave it; and he was a pensioner upon me till he died. Do not think that I take credit for this. I paid him to keep my secret, and to hold his tongue when the name of Pierrepoint was uttered in his hearing. A few days after my father-in-law's visit, I received another visitor in the person of Mrs. Fane. For two minutes after she had entered the room, I believed that my wife was standing before me: and it was only when I looked at the card which had been put into my hand that I knew who my visitor was. She too had heard of my good fortune, and came to appeal to me in behalf of her sister.

"I listened to her patiently, even when she uttered such phrases as 'remorse for the dreadful past,' 'the deepest penitence that ever a woman felt,' the 'mad mistake of an ill-directed mind.' I let her say these things. I was patient even when she hinted at forgiveness; though I knew what, in her mind, forgiveness meant. Forgiveness! I hoped she might be able to tell me something of Arthur Holroyde; but she could tell me nothing, except that he and her sister had parted in Buenos Ayres, and that the woman who had been my wife had found herself penniless and friendless in a strange city, and had been glad to come back to England as maid to a lady making the homeward passage. Mrs. Fane tried to make me believe that this separation had been a voluntary act on the part of her sister. I did not dispute the fact.

"In answer to Mrs. Fane's appeal, I told her that I was willing to allow my wife an income which would enable her to live in comfort and respectability; on the understanding that she should for ever abandon the name of Pierrepoint, and all claim to any family connection therewith; and that she should promise to reside abroad, where her name and her story would be alike unknown. I explained to my sister-in-law how easily I could obtain a divorce, had I chosen to endure the scandal attached to it, but that I did not so choose. I told her that the income allowed to her sister should be seven hundred and fifty pounds a-year—the half of my own income; and that if ever I succeeded to a larger fortune, I would double that allowance, always supposing that Caroline Pierrepoint led a creditable life, and kept the secret of her relationship to me. These conditions were very readily agreed to by Mrs. Fane on the part of her sister, and in the course of a few days the matter was entirely settled. I placed the business in the hands of a solicitor whom I could trust, and who did not know the real name of the Mrs. Howell to whom he sent a quarterly letter of credit on a foreign banker. Mrs. Fane and her sister departed for the Continent as soon as the arrangements had been completed, and I started for Marseilles on the first stage of my African expedition.

"From that time until the night on which I crossed the threshold of Scarsdale Hermitage, the story of my life has been a history of lonely wanderings in desolate and dangerous places. There are few spots beyond the ken of common travellers which are not familiar to me; there are few latitudes in which I have not lain down to rest with my gun by my side, and with my life in some measure depending on the punctuality with which I replenished the blaze that scared savage beasts and deadly reptiles from my lonely lair. For fifteen years I was a wanderer on the face of the earth. A letter reached me now and then from home. My own letters bore some record of my adventures back to the home in which my absence was so bitter a sorrow. I thank God even now that neither my father nor my mother ever knew the cause of my wandering life. They believed that I was possessed by a mania for perilous travel; and they lived and died in the expectation that I should return and settle down into an orthodox Pierrepoint at last. My father's death made me one of the richest men in the North Riding; and the mail that brought me tidings of his loss brought me also a letter from Mrs. Fane, claiming on her sister's behalf the increased income I had promised on my inheritance of Pierrepoint. In the course of my exile I met a man who had known Leonora Fane in Bengal; and from him I heard how base and treacherous a creature I had admitted into my home when I welcomed my wife's sister. From him I heard that Colonel Fane, infinitely wiser than myself, had carried the story of his wrongs into the House of Commons, and had set himself free from a wretched wife. After this, I thought a little more mercifully of the woman who had been my wife, and was inclined to believe her the weak victim of an evil counsellor, rather than the defiant sinner I had once considered her.

"Pity me, Marcia, if you can. I have told you the story of my life; but the story of my heart and mind would be too long, too dreary for telling. Until I saw you, I bore my burden patiently. Since then—— No, I have no right to speak of myself since then.

"I shall go back to my old existence. Nature, the old comforter, shall take me back to her giant arms. I will not ask you to forget me. I entreat you only to forgive me; and to remember that there is no hour of the day or night in which you do not occupy the thoughts of a man in whose desolate heart every thought of you shapes itself into a prayer."

CHAPTER VIII.

"AND YET MY DAYS GO ON, GO ON."

MARCIA DENISON read the last line of Godfrey Pierrepoint's confession with the summer dawn upon her face, and the fresh breath of the morning breeze blowing in upon her through the open windows. Throughout that dreary record of a blighted life no tear of hers had fallen on the page; but at the last—at the very last—her eyes grew dim, and two big drops rolled slowly down her cheeks and fell on that passage in which the wanderer promised to think of her and pray for her.

And from this moment all was over. The brief romance of her life closed with the close of Godfrey Pierrepoint's story. Henceforward he was to be a wanderer upon this earth, and she was not even to know the scene of his wandering. He was to die alone and friendless, and she had no hope of knowing either the hour or the place of his death. While she fancied him oppressed by the suffocating blasts of the desert, he might be freezing in the awful solitude of the arctic zone; while she thought of him as a living presence, he might be lying dead in the trackless depths of some tropical forest, with foul crawling creatures eating their way into his heart.

She was never to see him any more. As she lay awake in the broad morning sunlight, her lips shaped themselves into the cruel phrase—Never more! never more! Her life, which had been elevated into a new existence by his affection, was to drop back into its old dull course; and the magical influence of his love, which had illumined the commonest things with a kind of radiance, was to fade out and leave all things upon this earth duller and drearier than they had been to her before. For a little time she thought of her loss and sorrow with a dull despair. It seemed as if the link between herself and Godfrey Pierrepoint had been something more than a mutual affection arising out of their own hearts alone. Her instinctive faith in him, her tender reverence for him, seemed to belong to something higher and holier than the every-day emotions of this common earth. She had permitted herself to think that Heaven had destined her to be this man's companion and consoler, and that the impulse which drew her towards him was an instinct implanted in her breast by her Creator: and having once given admission to this thought, the foolish fancy had absorbed her mind—for it is so sweet to believe that our own happiness is a predestined joy, which we have only to receive in unquestioning thankfulness. And after having indulged this delicious fancy, the pain of an irrevocable parting was very bitter. A widow mourning for her lost husband could scarcely have suffered a keener sorrow than that which bowed Marcia Denison's head as the slow days that carried Godfrey Pierrepoint farther away from her wore themselves wearily out.

But she bore her sorrow with a meek heroism, which was an attribute of her character. She had been so accustomed to be sorrowful, and to keep the secret of her grief. Even those who knew her best had no suspicion of the truth.

Sir Jasper flung the burden of fatherly anxiety upon his medical man as coolly as he flung his business-letters to the solicitor who answered them.

"My daughter is not herself, Mr. Redmond," he said to the respectable old family-surgeon, who had inspected the Baronet's tongue with the same aspect of mournful earnestness, and sighed the same plaintive little sigh over the Baronet's pulse three times a week for the last twelve months; "and I really do beg that you will make a point of seeing that she becomes herself at the earliest opportunity. She's as gray and chalky as a third-rate portrait in the Royal Academy. Can't you warm her up a little with some nice yellows— tonics, I should say?"

The surgeon shook his head.

"There is a want of tone, Sir Jasper," he murmured; "an evident want of tone."

"Of course there is, man," answered the Baronet peevishly; "I can see that as well as you can; and there used to be a good deal of feeling in those cool pearly grays of hers. She doesn't complain, and she's very attentive to me, and reads and sings to me; but there's an unsteadiness in her upper notes that I don't at all like; and, in short, if you can't bring her round, I must really take her up to London and get her brought round by somebody there."

The surgeon did his best, and Marcia obeyed him as meekly as a child. He told Miss Denison that her father had expressed considerable uneasiness about her altered looks, and this influenced her. She felt a faint thrill of pleasure in the thought that her father cared for her a little; perhaps, after all, just enough to make him uneasy when she was ill, and anxious that she should recover. After this little interview with the surgeon she made a sublime effort, and thrust her grief as much aside as any deathless sorrow can be thrust by a constant mourner. She had no hope that her burden would ever be less. Her only prayer was, that she might daily learn to bear it better, and that the life which was valueless to herself might be of use to other people.

And so her life resumed its old course. She spent her lonely mornings in her own room—sometimes at her piano, sometimes with her books, still oftener at her easel; and Art, the divine consoler, lightened the burden of her desolate hours and deadened the sting of her grief. In the afternoons she went on her old rounds amongst her poor, with Dorothy and a Mount-Saint-Bernard dog for her companions; and it was in these afternoon walks that she most sharply felt the loss of her only friend. She passed the Hermitage now and then, and looked sadly at the closed casements. Dorothy's grandmother still kept watch and ward in the lonely cottage; for by a strange caprice Sir Jasper's tenant had not abandoned his tenancy, but had engaged himself to send the Baronet's agent a half-yearly cheque for the rent.

"Which proves that he intends to come back sooner or later," said the Baronet.

But Marcia, pondering on this fact, fancied it was just possible that Godfrey Pierrepoint had some tender reverence for the place in which he had known and loved her, and wished to keep his hearth sacred from the presence of strangers.

"If I were wandering far away in savage places, it would please me to think there was one spot kept empty for my coming back, even if I knew in my own heart that I never could go back to occupy it," she thought sadly.

And out of her fancy there arose a pale vision of the future; and she saw Godfrey Pierrepoint coming back, after many years, old and gray and tired, to sit by the old hearth, and to look from the old casement at trees that had been underwood when he first looked out upon them. And he would come to the Abbey with the thought of seeing her, and would hear perhaps that she had been lying for years in the vault under Scarsdale chancel. Or she might live to be old and gray herself, and would meet him perhaps some day in the glade, where they had fled together from the storm; meet him so changed a creature that the passionate sorrow of to-day would seem a thing to talk of with an incredulous smile.

"Do our souls really die before we do?" she

thought wonderingly. "It must be so sad to outlive oneself."

Sir Jasper was very much inclined to resent his tenant's departure, and quoted Voltaire and Diderot to an alarming extent upon the subject.

"I like the man and the man's society, and I consider it a very churlish act on the man's part to turn his back upon me. 'Virtue,' Diderot remarks, 'under whatever phase we contemplate it, is a sacrifice of self;' and, upon my word, Marcia, I consider Pauncefort a very selfish fellow."

For some time the Baronet bewailed his friend. He was more than usually polite to his daughter; he was cordial; he was affectionate even: but every evening Marcia became more aware that there was something wanting to her father's complete satisfaction. He grew tired of *écarté;* he yawned drearily in the midst of the most exquisite passages Beethoven ever wrote; he trifled discontentedly with the leaves of his *Saturday;* he quarrelled with the opinions of his *Times;* quoted Voltaire to the effect that modern writers are only contortionists; he recited the most peevish sentences in *Hamlet;* and found fault with the colouring of his favourite Etty.

Miss Denison was unselfishly anxious for her father's comfort, and watched him closely; but she could imagine neither a reason nor a remedy for his discontent. One day, however, the enigma was suddenly solved by the Baronet himself.

"Thank you, my love," he murmured drowsily, as Marcia played the last bar of a sonata; "very sweet indeed. You manage those cinquepated passages remarkably well; but I don't think your general time was quite as smooth as I have heard it. You miss some one to play duets with you. Suppose we ask the widow to come back to us for a week or two? We're under a kind of engagement to have her back, you know; and the sooner we get it over and have done with it, the better."

Sir Jasper cleared his throat with a little rasping cough, and peered furtively above the edge of his *Times* in a timid survey of his daughter's face.

She did not receive his proposition at all rapturously.

"Do you really want to have Mrs. Harding back, papa?" she asked wonderingly.

"*I* want her back, my dear Marcia! What can I want with a florid widow?" cried the Baronet. "But we asked her for the autumn; and having done so, of course we're in for it. *Noblesse oblige*, you know, my love; and so on. A florid widow for the autumn may be a nuisance; but having invited her, you're bound to have her."

"The autumn, papa!" exclaimed Marcia. "You said a week or two just now."

"Unquestionably, my dear, and I mean a week or two; but the autumn is a more gentlemanly way of putting it. You can't serve out your hospitality by the week, as if it were rations. You'd better write to Mrs. Harding to-morrow, and tell her that autumn is close at hand, and we are looking out for her promised visit."

"Do you think there is any necessity to write, papa? Depend upon it, if Mrs. Harding wishes to come back, she'll propose coming of her own accord, as she did before."

"And then we have all the worry of receiving her without the credit of inviting her! My dear Marcia, you have not the faintest idea of diplomacy."

Miss Denison was silent for some minutes, during which Sir Jasper still watched her across the upper edge of his newspaper, and then she said gravely:

"Papa, the honest truth is, that I don't like Mrs. Harding."

"My love, did I ever ask you to like her? I only ask you to perform your part of the engagement you made with her."

"*I* made, papa! It was you who asked her to come back, not I."

"Indeed!" exclaimed the Baronet innocently. "*I* asked her, did I? I suppose I found myself pushed into a kind of conversational corner, and was obliged to say something civil."

Marcia grew very thoughtful. A light was beginning to dawn faintly upon her mind; a light that showed her something very unpleasant—the image of her father beguiled and entrapped by a false and mercenary adventuress.

"Papa," she said, after a brief silence, "I don't think Mrs. Harding is a good woman."

"No more do I, my love," Sir Jasper answered promptly. "I don't presume to form any opinion upon the subject. How should I? I've never yet been able to come to any decision about Mary Stuart, and I know a great deal more about her than ever I shall know of Mrs. Harding. How difficult it is to have a decided opinion about anybody! There have been people who have called Queen Elizabeth 'a sad dog;' there are people who swear by her cousin as a persecuted divinity. All the light thrown upon the subject by contending historians is not strong enough to reveal it to every one in the same colours. How do I know whether Mrs. Harding is 'good' or 'bad'? I know that her gowns are made by a Frenchwoman, and that she is past mistress in the science of putting on a tight glove. I know that her voice is harmonious, and her presence agreeable to the eye; that she neither drops her *h*'s, nor bangs my doors. For the rest, I neither know nor seek to know any thing. What can be the good of discussing the moral attributes of an acquaintance, when you live in a world which would not allow you to know a John Howard or a Captain Coram if he eat peas with his knife?"

There were few subjects which Marcia had ever disputed with her father; but she knew him well enough to know the utter uselessness of any discussion when his own pleasure was involved in the argument.

"If you tell me to write to Mrs. Harding, I shall obey you, papa," she said with a half-suppressed sigh; "but her visit will give me any thing but pleasure; and I should be very glad if you had opened your doors to worthier acquaintance. The old county people—"

"The old county people would come to me in state, and bore me out of my life," answered the Baronet testily. "What have I in common with the old county families? I don't hunt; and in the finest run that your hunting fellows ever bragged of, my sympathies would be with the fox rather than the whooping idiots who expend such an unnecessary amount of perspiration in pursuing him. I am neither horsy nor doggy; I am neither agricultural nor philanthropic. I should scarcely know the difference between a short-legged Galway hunter and the purest Arab that ever bounded free upon his native plains. I know no more of ploughing by machinery or sub-soil drainage than an Icelander. I know nothing about the dwellings of the working-classes; except that, as they don't interest themselves about my dwelling, and wouldn't drive a nail into a window-sash, or sweep away a handful of shavings for me without being paid for their trouble, they can scarcely expect me to interest myself in their comfort without being paid for my trouble. So you see, Marcia, the county families and I could only bore one another; and you can't give a whole houseful of people to understand that they're a collective nuisance without running some risk of offending them. With Mrs. Harding, on the contrary, I am safe. The woman knows how to make herself agreeable; and what is better still, she knows when she is making herself agreeable, and when she isn't. There is no creature so fascinating as the woman who knows when she's a nuisance. So I think, my dear, you had better write to the widow to-morrow morning, as you proposed," concluded Sir Jasper, artfully ducking behind his *Times*, and avoiding any encounter of glances with his daughter.

Marcia wrote the obnoxious letter as uncomplainingly as if she had been a child; but it was very coldly worded. "Papa wishes me to remind you that you proposed paying us a visit in the autumn"—"Papa will be very glad to see you, if your plans will allow of your coming to us;" and so on ran the letter. There was no word of friendship from Marcia herself, no hint that her own pleasure would be enhanced by the lady's visit. Miss Denison could not forget that the widow had traduced Godfrey Pierrepoint, and she could not forgive the vague slander. Now that she was familiar with the history of his life, she wondered how and when this woman had known him. The record of his youth was the record of a life spent in seclusion. In all the story there was no mention of friends or even acquaintance. How could Mrs. Harding have encountered the hard-working literary hack whose days had been spent in the solitude of his chambers? Marcia concluded that the widow's acquaintance with Mr. Pierrepoint could only have arisen through his sister-in-law, Leonora Fane, and that she had been amongst Mrs. Fane's visitors at the Camberwell cottage. As Mrs. Fane's friend, it was very likely that Mrs. Harding might have heard Godfrey Pierrepoint vilified and traduced, since the only possible defence of the wife must involve the blackening of the husband's character. But how could this explanation account for the widow's apparent agitation when she had recognised Godfrey? This question perplexed Miss Denison; but then she suspected that it was very possible she had been mistaken as to Mrs. Harding's manner.

It was towards the end of August that Miss Denison wrote to the Circe who had contrived to make her society necessary to Sir Jasper; and in less than a week she received the widow's answer, which was to the effect that Mrs. Harding *had* made other plans for the autumn; but since dear Sir Jasper was good enough to remind her of her half-implied promise to return, and since there was no house in which she was so happy as in the dear old abbey, and no society so intellectual and improving as dear Sir Jasper's, she would forego all other engagements and follow the dictates of her own inclination, which prompted her to come back to Scarsdale.

Marcia sighed as she handed her father the widow's epistle.

"Don't you see that it's a false letter, papa?" she said, almost impatiently; "made up of conventional sentences, as artificial and meaningless as if it were copied out of a Complete Letter-writer."

"Of course it is, my dear," the Baronet answered with perfect good-humour. "Mrs. Harding is conventional; Mrs. Harding is artificial. Do you think if she were not, that I would allow you to invite her here? If she were original, I would have nothing to do with her; for originality is only a milder name for eccentricity. I suppose Paunecfort sets up for originality; and look at his conduct. What can be more disgustingly selfish than his rushing away at the very time I most required his society? Don't bury yourself in that Crome when I'm speaking to you, pray, Marcia; it's a charming little bit I know, but you can bury yourself in it on a more fitting occasion. I was about to remark that conventionality is a very desirable quality in an acquaintance; and Mrs. Harding's letter is extremely nice —six 'dear Sir Jaspers' on the two pages. But I suppose your candid person would have called me 'that brute Sir Jasper;' or 'your preposterous old father;' or 'the governor;' or 'the middle-aged party;' or something equally abusive."

CHAPTER IX.

TWOPENNY-POSTMAN.

It is not to be supposed that Mr. Dobb and his circle confined their social intercourse entirely to the Sunday-evening reunions at the house of the brewer's-clerk. There were grand occasions on which Henry Adolphus and his associates enjoyed themselves in a more elaborate manner; and on such occasions Selina would generally invite her rustic cousin to join in the festivities. For when you are about to regale your friends, a farm-bailiff's daughter, who can bring you a hamper of eggs and poultry, fruit and vegetables, home-cured bacon, and odorous virgin honey, is not a person to be disregarded.

There was very brilliant weather during the last weeks of August; and inspired by the breath of balmy breezes that blew into the windows of Amanda Villas, only a little tainted by the sulphurous vapours of a neighbouring brick-field, Mr. Dobb set himself to work to organise a picnic.

The idea was discussed on the first Sunday evening after it had sprung, complete as Minerva, from the lively Dobb's brain.

"Suppose we fix on the first. The bloated aristocrat will be marking the harmless partridge with his cruel eye, and why should not we also have our little game?" exclaimed Henry Adolphus. "Spinner, my boy, just take your pencil and jot down a few figures. We'll do the thing in slap-up style, or we'll leave it undone. First and foremost, where shall we go?"

Of course every body suggested a different place, and pooh-poohed his neighbour's suggestion. But the brewer's-clerk was the despot of his small circle; and after allowing his guests to contradict one another until the argumentative was verging upon the quarrelsome, Mr. Dobb arose, in all the majesty of the master-spirit, and spread the oil of conciliation upon the troubled waters of contention.

"Don't cut one another's throats just yet," he exclaimed; "if you don't respect the laws of your country, you may as well have mercy on my wife's kidderminster. I'll tell you what it is, we will not go to Mildale Abbey, Spinner, for if we do we shall make Poeombe savage; and we won't go to Bray Common, Poeombe, for fear of infuriating Spinner; and if we were to choose Waldon Woods, as Smith proposes, we should bring down upon our heads the wrath of Sanders, who votes for Turlingdon Meads. Our motto shall be *Pax vobiscum*. We won't aggravate any body by obliging any body else. We'll go to the Lemley Hills, which not one of you duffers has had the good taste to remember, and which is the finest picnic place in the county, and five hundred feet above the level of the dome of St. Paul's."

"Oh, Selina," whispered Dorothy, who was sitting near her cousin, "do you think Henry Adolphus will let *me* go?"

Mr. Dobb's sharp ear caught the whisper.

"There's my cousin Dorothy bribing my wife to give her an invitation," said the clerk. "No, Dorothy; not six pair of fowls, as you generously propose to contribute; we'll say a couple of couple of fowls, and a ditto ditto of ducks, and any small trifle in the way of a twenty-pound ham, or a round of corned beef, that you may wish to throw in."

"I'm sure father would let me bring a hamper," gasped Dorothy, looking at Mr. Catheron, who sat by her side pulling fiercely at a big cigar, and who evinced very little interest in the picnic proposition. "You'll go, won't you, Gervoise?" she whispered. "I don't care a bit about going, unless you are to be there."

"Dorothy!" cried Mr. Dobb sternly, "this is *not* leap-year; and matrimonial proposals emanating from the fair sex are as unwarrantable as they are uncalled for. Besides which, whispering is not permitted in polite society. However, your youth and ignorance shall plead your excuse, and you may consider yourself forgiven."

After this Mr. Dobb and his friends went into

some very elaborate calculations of ways and means: how Mr. Spinner was to bring his wife and sister and a gigantic veal-and-ham pie; Mr. Smith his niece and two bottles of the best Old Tom from the Castleford Arms; Mr. Pocombe was to be accompanied by Mrs. Pocombe and a cold saddle of mutton; Mr. Sanders, being a bachelor, was taxed lightly, to the extent of a bottle of sherry and a plum-cake, to be bought at the pastry-cook's.

"And no black-beetles in it, if you please!" Mr. Dobb interjected earnestly. "It is not generally known that the rich appearance of wedding-cakes is produced by black-beetles and London porter; but it is a melancholy fact, nevertheless. So please be careful, Sanders; we won't say any thing about bad eggs or rancid butter, for those of course are used by all confectioners."

Mr. Dobb himself proposed to contribute what he called sundries, and which seemed to consist chiefly of such inexpensive elements of the feast as salt, pepper, mustard, and pickles; but which the dictatorial Dobb declared "would cost a precious sight more than any body would imagine."

"And what will you bring, my honourable friend in the most popular branch of the two services?" asked the brewer's-clerk, turning suddenly to Gervoise Catheron, whose dark brows contracted gloomily as he sat puffing slowly at his cigar, with his head bent and his face in shadow. "Come, you're the heaviest swell amongst us, and you ought to come out strong. What are you going to stand for the commonweal?—Mind your pie isn't common weal, by the way, Spinner."

"I don't know that I shall be able to go to your confounded picnic," answered the sub-lieutenant sulkily. "In the first place, I detest all picnics; and in the second place, I may be on duty."

"And in the third place, you don't care about the expense," returned Mr. Dobb with a sneer. "Who talks of the extravagant habits of the army and navy? Here's a gentleman who has so great a respect for the image of his sovereign, that he shirks his friends for the sake of saving half-a-dozen impressions of her 'picture in little.'"

"Oh, confound your picnic!" cried the lieutenant. "If it's my contribution you want, you're welcome to it whether I go or stay away. I suppose a sovereign will shut up your insolence—eh, Dobb?"

"I suppose it will," answered that gentleman, "when I get it."

These last four words were pronounced with *intention*. Gervoise Catheron felt in his pockets, and the frown upon his handsome dissolute face grew darker than before. He had trusted in Mr. Dobb's indignant repudiation of his offer, and found himself in an unpleasant position, exposed to all the insolence that can be expressed by half-a-dozen pairs of under-bred eyes and half-a-dozen under-bred tongues.

When the descendent of a good old family keeps low company, he generally has to pay very dearly for his predilection. Oh, most fatal of all vices that can lead a man to his ruin: the bane of a Brauwer and a Morland, the destruction of a

Savage and a Burns! Unhappy is the hour in which ambitious youth first exclaims that it is better to reign in a village than to serve in Rome.

While the lieutenant's frown deepened and the grin upon the half-dozen vulgar faces grew broader, a little hand crept stealthily into Gervoise Catheron's palm,—a tender little hand, soft and gentle as the fluttering of a pigeon's wing,— and the lieutenant felt the pressure of a coin—a coin which he grasped as eagerly as the traditional drowning man may have grasped the traditional straw,—and in whose touch and weight he recognised a sovereign. Dorothy had been groping in her pocket for the purse in which she kept one glittering golden piece, very much on the same principle as that on which the Miss Primroses kept their wealth; and she was ineffably happy in being able to relieve her lover's embarrassment.

Mr. Catheron flung down the sovereign with such an impetus that it spun upon the table with a loud ringing noise before it settled in the very centre of the hospitable board and under the shadow of the mighty can that contained the customary gallon.

"Corn in Egypt!" cried Mr. Spinner, a little disappointed by the unlooked-for *dénouement.*

"And a good one," said Mr. Dobb.

"I'm sure the lieutenant couldn't have acted more liberal," added the pacific Selina, who, in her own words, was always anxious to make things pleasant.

"And now I'll wish you good-evening, gentlemen," said Mr. Catheron, throwing the end of his cigar across Mr. Spinner's sandy head in its way to the open window, and kicking over the chair from which he had risen as he walked to the door. "I've paid my share towards your very hospitable entertainment, and you and your picnic may be ——!"

"Come, I say," exclaimed Dobb, pocketing the sovereign, "this won't do, you know, Catheron. A lark is a lark, you know; and a man who can't stand a little good-natured chaff had better turn hermit at once and shut himself for ever from his fellow-man. Sit down, can't you, old fellow, and have another weed?—Here, Spinner, give the lieutenant one of those regalias of yours; never mind if they're sixpence each, we'll subscribe a penny all round and pay you for it," added the clerk, in whose circle playful allusions to the state of a man's finances or his unwillingness to part with his money were considered immensely amusing.

The lieutenant complied sulkily, and resumed his seat sulkily, and accepted Mr. Spinner's cigar as ungraciously as he accepted every other civility that evening. Dorothy looked at him with hopeless, despairing eyes. She had a dim idea that he was a worthless creature, and that only misery and disappointment could come of her love for him; and yet the most transient look from his dark haggard eyes, the faintest touch of his weak womanish hand, moved her with a thrill of emotion that was more like pain than joy in its intensity.

Mr. Catheron had of late submitted to a good deal of that elephantine badinage which Mr. Dobb called chaff, but which less facetiously-disposed people might have considered vulgar insolence. "Heavy swell" though the lieutenant might be in the estimation of the Dobb circle, he was fain to play second fiddle, and to give way upon most points to the brewer's-clerk. Sooth to say, Gervoise Catheron was in the clerk's power, bound to him by the most ignoble bondage that can make one man the slave of another. He owed Mr. Dobb money. The system which had begun with the borrowing of "a little silver," or half-a-sovereign, had gone on for the last six months, and by this time Gervoise Catheron owed the brewer's-clerk upwards of thirty pounds. Now the value of money is purely relative; and thirty pounds—which might seem the merest bagatelle to a man who paid income-tax for two or three thousand per annum—is a large sum when subtracted from the funds of an individual who has only a hundred and twenty pounds a year for board, washing, lodging, and clothing, *menus plaisirs* and servant's wages. The thirty pounds had constituted the balance of a little fund which Henry Adolphus had hoarded in his bachelor-days, and the greater part of which had been expended on the furnishing of the newly-built dovecot to which he had brought his Selina. The thirty pounds had constituted the nucleus of a future fortune; and Mrs. Dobb fondly believed that it still stood to her husband's credit in the Roxborough Savings-Bank. Supreme as the facetious Dobb might be among his companions, and meekly as his wife's white eyelashes drooped under his noble gaze, there were matters which he did not care to reveal to that amiable partner; and this little affair of the thirty pounds was one of them.

"I should have to stand no end of nagging if I told her," soliloquised Mr. Dobb; "and nagging won't get the money back from Catheron."

It is not to be supposed that a gentleman of Mr. Dobb's business capacity would have been so weak as to lend his friend money without a view to ultimate profit. The clerk's advances were only so many investments of capital—investments that promised to bring in very handsome interest. The precept laid down by the warrior Duke of Wellington with regard to good interest and bad security, although as nearly infallible as human wisdom can be, is apt to be overlooked by the sanguine capitalist, in whom nature has implanted the genius of the speculator. For every five pounds which Mr. Dobb had advanced to the lieutenant, he held that gentleman's I O U for ten. No Catheron ever stopped to count the cost of any personal gratification; and Gervoise was as willing to promise a hundred per cent as he would have been to promise five for the accommodation he required. When a man has a shrewd suspicion that his I O U is only worth the half-sheet of paper on which it is written, he is apt to be very indifferent as to the sum for which he writes himself down a debtor.

Gervoise Catheron met all his friend's remonstrances with the assurance that the money should be paid, principal and interest, every sixpence. The lieutenant had been a gambler in a small way ever since he had been old enough to read the sporting intelligence in his father's papers, and to go shares in the half-crown which a neighbouring butcher's boy adventured on the Derby favourite.

He had loitered at the corner of Farringdon Street, and hung about the purlieus of Leather Lane, and lounged against posts, and besotted himself with beer in the dusky parlours of sporting publics in Newgate Market, in the intervals of freedom which his profession had afforded him; and even now, when his regiment was stationed at Castleford, he went up to London whenever he could get a day's leave, and went sneaking back to his old haunts, to meet the same seedy conspirators at the same street-corners, and to hold stealthy consultations in the same undertones, and with the same air of plotting an assassination or so.

Again and again he assured Mr. Dobb that the flimsy little I O U's, scrawled so carelessly in the weak illegible hand, should be faithfully redeemed. Henry Adolphus knew all his schemes; his secret intelligence about the outsider that was to win the Two Thousand, and didn't; his equally reliable information respecting the dark horse from Yorkshire, which had been artfully reported lame, but which was known by the deep ones to be a flyer, and was a safe winner for the Chester Cup. As the scent of blood to the beast of prey, so is the slang of the turf to weak mankind. The love of horse-racing seems to be innate in the human breast. There is no fascination so irresistible as the atmosphere of the betting-ring; no intoxication so overpowering as the excitement of the race-course; and no subtle amalgamation of southern blossoms that Mr. Rimmel can devise will ever be as popular as the simple perfume which he calls Jockey Club.

Henry Adolphus, trembling for his thirty pounds, was yet weak enough to heed the voice of the charmer, and to believe again and again in the reliable information, which always resulted in discomfiture. The two men studied Holt's betting-lists until the flimsy paper on which the price-current of the ring was printed grew soft and flabby with much folding and unfolding. They discussed the prospects of the racing-season until poor Selina's shallow brain grew confused with their stable-jargon; but the more they talked the deeper sank the feet of the brewer's-clerk into that fatal quagmire which men call the turf. There were times when, instead of regretting his folly in having lent money to Catheron, Mr. Dobb bewailed his inability to speculate on his own account, so brilliant seemed the opportunity for speculation, so certain appeared the prospect of success. The better part of the racing-year had gone by; hope and despair had reigned alternately in Gervoise Catheron's breast. The Two Thousand and the One Thousand, the Metropolitan, the Derby, the Oaks, the Ascot Stakes and Cup, the Liverpool Plate, the Chester Cup, the Great Ebor,—all the grand spring and summer races had gone by; and Gervoise Catheron, backing outsiders with the desperate tenacity of a man who wants to win a large stake with the smallest capital, had lost his pitiful ventures one after another, borrowing wherever he could borrow, and pawning whatever he had to pawn, until at last the great autumnal contest was near at hand, and the sporting universe began to talk about The Leger, the grand encounter of the year—the battle-ground where Greek meets Greek, and comes the tug of war which is perhaps to win the blue ribbon of the North for the victor of Epsom Downs or the conqueror of Newmarket.

The end of August was fast approaching, and from the end of August to the fifteenth of September was an interval only too brief for action; but as yet the lieutenant had not been able to raise a sixpence for a venture which he declared and believed might redeem the fortunes of the year. He knew the state of his friend Dobb's finances well enough to know that any appeal in that quarter would be fruitless. He had borrowed of his brother officers, and had sunk to the lowest depths of that degradation into which the habitual borrower, who never repays, must ultimately go down. He was in debt to all the tradesmen with whom he had any dealings; for small loans of money as well as for goods. Even poor little Dorothy's savings had not been sacred for him; and the sovereign produced for the picnic had been the last of a little hoard contained in a pasteboard Swiss cottage, which the faithful little maid had ruthlessly broken into for her lover's benefit. And in the only sporting-circle to which Mr. Catheron had access there was no such thing as credit. The bookmen with whom he had dealings sat in dingy parlours, with canvas-bags before them, and received the golden tribute of their votaries as fast as they could count the coins handed in to them.

The lieutenant grew moodier and moodier as the days went by, and no glimmer from the polestar of hope lighted the dull horizon. And this time his information was so certain — this time there could be no chance of disappointment. The knowing ones were all agreed for once in a way; and the voices of Farringdon Street and Newgate Market were as the voice of one man.

"If I had a million of money, I'd put every stiver of it on Twopenny-Postman; and as much more as I could beg or borrow into the bargain. If any body would lay me a pony against my grandmother, I'd put her on, and not be afraid of the old lady coming to grief," had been heard to exclaim a gentleman of the blue-apron profession, who was the oracle of his circle, and whose lightest word was absorbed by eager listeners, and fondly dwelt upon in future converse. A fortune was to be made by Twopenny-Postman, said the lieutenant's advisers; if a man only had a ten-pound note or so wherewith to venture. But Gervoise Catheron had neither "tenner" nor "fiver," as he said plaintively to his friend Dobb; and the chance would be lost.

The two men talked the affair over as they walked back to Castleford in the starlight that autumn evening, after escorting little Dorothy to the gates of Scarsdale.

"There never was such a chance," said Mr. Catheron. "The horse has been kept out of the way all this season; and as he never did much when he was a two-year-old, the public ain't sweet upon him. But I think they ought to have had a sickener of your crack two-year-olds by this time, after the way they burnt their fingers with Prometheus for the Two Thousand; he beat every thing that was out on the T. Y. C. last year, and shut up like a telescope in the great race. Your crack two-year-olds are like your

Infant Rosciuses and your precocious children whose names are Norval at three years old, and who don't know B from a bull's foot at twenty. Twopenny-Postman is a great ugly rawboned animal with a stride from here to yonder; and he hasn't been kept out of the way for nothing. Those who saw him run on the Curragh say his rush at the finish was just as if he'd been shot out of a gun. He's a Yorkshire horse, and he's entered under the name of Smithson; but there's three men interested in him. They know all about him in Hull. There's a publican, called Howden, has got a third share in him; and I know something of Howden. He's a deep one, is Howden. He and his chums have been backing the horse on the quiet ever since the spring. You could have had any odds a month or two ago; the swells are all on Lord Edinbro and Mr. Cheerful; and Twopenny-Postman hasn't been inquired for any where till very lately. But he's been creeping up in the Manchester betting; they know what's what at Manchester, and you won't get more than fifteen to one; but even at that your 'tenner' will bring you in a hundred and fifty, and that's not bad interest for your money."

Mr. Dobb's mouth watered as the mouth of an epicure who hears the eloquent description of some impossible banquet. If the lieutenant had been able to back Twopenny-Postman and had won a hundred and fifty, the I O U's which now seemed such miserable scraps of wastepaper might be converted into crisp bank-notes. Ah, then, what triumph to go to Selina and say, " Behold the fruits of a prudent investment!" and he would be able to give her a new bonnet, and to treat himself to gorgeous velvet raiment, such as he had beheld with envy on the stalwart backs of the military dandies lounging in the Castleford High Street; and after doing this, he might still put fifty pounds in the bank in place of the abstracted thirty.

But then he had trusted in the voice of the lieutenant before to-day. How about the other outsiders in which Mr. Catheron had so confidently believed? How about Hydrophobia and Rhadamanthus, Mixed Biscuits, Newgate Calendar, and Alcibiades? all of whom had been represented to him as infallible,—all of whom had suffered ignominious defeat. Common-sense whispered to the brewer's-clerk that Gervoise Catheron's information was a delusion and a snare; but the demon of speculation possessed himself of Mr. Dobb's other ear, and reminded him that a man cannot go on losing for ever, and that a speculator who has made half-a-dozen unlucky strokes is very likely to make a great *coup* on the seventh venture. Nor was Mr. Catheron himself slow to make use of this argument.

"Suppose Sir Josiah Morley had left off betting when he lost twenty thou. upon Skeleton," said the lieutenant, "where would he be now? Suppose Mr. Cheerful had given up training after the defeat of Gutta-Percha, the colt he gave two thousand five hundred for as a yearling? The secret of success on the turf is persistence; and the man who goes on long enough is sure to make a fortune. I know we've been deuced unlucky all the summer; but the tip I've got this time comes from a new quarter, and I know it's a safe quarter. However, say no more about it. I've got no money, and you can't lend me any, or get any body else to lend me any; so that settles the question."

But the question was by no means to be set at rest thus easily. The image of the ugly rawboned horse haunted Mr. Dobb in the dead of the night, and his rest was broken by the visions of financial triumphs that might have been his if he had possessed a ten-pound note. Five pounds advanced to Catheron would have recompensed that gentleman for his information, and would have brought him in seventy-five pounds, out of which Henry Adolphus would have claimed sixty. With the other five the clerk could have speculated on his own account, and would have stood to win another seventy-five; and by this means the sixteenth of September would have beheld him possessed of a hundred and thirty-five pounds —the nucleus of a colossal fortune. Had Lafitte as much with which to begin his mighty career? Tumbling his long greasy hair feverishly upon what seemed a peculiarly lumpy pillow, Mr. Dobb beheld himself in a brilliant future; doing little bills for the Castleford officers at thirty per cent, and renewing them for another fifteen. Nor was the range of his mind's eye limited to this glowing vision: far away in the immeasurable distance of dreamland, he saw the image of a man leaning against a pillar of the Stock Exchange, while his fellow men gazed reverently on his rhadamanthine countenance as if they would therefrom divine the secrets of empires—and the name of that man was Dobb.

The clerk went to his office, looking pale and flabby of aspect, the next morning; and writing to a customer on business connected with the brewery, he found himself beginning:

. "We take the Twopenny-Postman to inform you that our X, XX, and XXX of last March are now," &c. &c.

END OF VOL. II.

LONDON:
ROBSON AND SON, GREAT NORTHERN PRINTING WORKS,
PANCRAS ROAD, N.W.